LOVE IS PATIENT

40 DEVOTIONAL GEMS AND BIBLE STUDY TRUTHS FROM PAUL'S LETTERS TO THE CORINTHIANS

40-DAY BIBLE STUDY SERIES
BOOK 7

PETER DEHAAN

Love Is Patient: 40 Devotional Gems and Bible Study Truths from Paul's Letters to the Corinthians Copyright © 2021 by Peter DeHaan.

40-Day Bible Study Series, Book 7

All rights reserved: No part of this book may be reproduced, disseminated, or transmitted in any form, by any means, or for any purpose without the express written consent of the author or his legal representatives. The only exception is short excerpts and the cover image for reviews or academic research. For permissions: peterdehaan.com/contact.

Unless otherwise noted, Scriptures taken from the Holy Bible, New International Version®, NIV®. Copyright © 1973, 1978, 1984, 2011 by Biblica, Inc.™ Used by permission of Zondervan. All rights reserved worldwide. www.zondervan.com The "NIV" and "New International Version" are trademarks registered in the United States Patent and Trademark Office by Biblica, Inc.™

Library of Congress Control Number: 2021914025

Published by Rock Rooster Books, Grand Rapids, Michigan

ISBN:

- 978-1-948082-64-8 (e-book)
- 978-1-948082-65-5 (paperback)
- 978-1-948082-66-2 (hardcover)

Credits:

- Developmental editor: Kathryn Wilmotte
- Copy editor/proofreader: Robyn Mulder
- Cover design: Taryn Nergaard
- Author photo: Chelsie Jensen Photography

To Kolby DeHaan

Series by Peter DeHaan

40-Day Bible Study Series takes a fresh and practical look into Scripture, book by book.

Bible Character Sketches Series celebrates people in Scripture, from the well-known to the obscure.

Holiday Celebration Bible Study Series rejoices in the holidays with Jesus.

Visiting Churches Series takes an in-person look at church practices and traditions to inform and inspire today's followers of Jesus.

Be the first to hear about Peter's new books and receive updates at PeterDeHaan.com/updates.

CONTENTS

Paul's Letters to Corinth	1
Day 1: No Divisions	5
Dig Deeper: The Dangers of Following Christian Celebrities	9
Day 2: Foolishness and Wisdom	13
Day 3: The Mind of Christ	17
Day 4: Baby Christians	21
Day 5: Worthy of Imitation	25
Day 6: Judge Others or Not	29
Dig Deeper: The Lost Letter	33
Day 7: Litigious Christians	37
Day 8: God's Temples	41
Day 9: Sex, Marriage, and Life	45
Day 10: Freedom in Jesus	49
Day 11: Run to Win	53
Day 12: The Temptation to Sin	57
Day 13: Flee from Idolatry	61
Dig Deeper: Judge	67
Day 14: Put Others First	71
Day 15: Interdependent	75
Day 16: An Unworthy Manner	79
Day 17: Thirteen Spiritual Gifts	83
Day 18: One Body United	87
Day 19: Love Is Patient	91
Day 20: The Greatest of These Is Love	95
Day 21: Build Up the Church	99
Day 22: When You Come Together	103

Day 23: Alive in Jesus	107
Dig Deeper: Can We Be Baptized for Dead People?	111
Day 24: Do God's Work	115
Day 25: If It's God's Will	119
Dig Deeper: A Holy Kiss	123
Day 26: When People Pray	127
Day 27: Restoration	131
Dig Deeper: Peddle God for Profit	135
Day 28: Freedom	139
Day 29: Easy or Hard?	143
Day 30: Live by Faith	147
Day 31: God's New Creation	151
Day 32: Paul's Commendation	155
Day 33: Yoked with Unbelievers	161
Day 34: Godly Sorrow	165
Day 35: Generosity	169
Dig Deeper: The Old Testament in 1 and 2 Corinthians	173
Day 36: A Cheerful Giver	177
Day 37: Take Every Thought Captive	181
Day 38: Devoted to Jesus	185
Dig Deeper: False Teachers	189
Day 39: Paul's Thorn in the Flesh	191
Dig Deeper: Encourage One Another	195
Day 40: Paul's Blessing	197
What Book Do You Want to Read Next?	201
For Small Groups, Sunday School, and Classes	203
If You're New to the Bible	205
About Peter DeHaan	209
Books by Peter DeHaan	211

PAUL'S LETTERS TO CORINTH

Paul (formerly called Saul) is a zealous Jew, pursuing his faith with full abandon. He sees the growing Jesus movement as an affront to his beliefs and seeks to squelch it. To do so, he harasses and hunts down Jesus's followers, arresting them and throwing them in jail.

Yet God has a different plan for Paul. This committed Jew has a supernatural encounter with Jesus on the road to Damascus and decides to follow him. He then goes all in for his Savior (see Acts 9:1–22).

Paul then travels the region, telling others the good news of salvation through Jesus. One place Paul visits is Corinth, located in what is modern-day Greece. He spends a year and a half there, teaching them about God and helping them grow in their faith. This is much longer than he spends in most of the other towns he visits.

You'd think that after investing eighteen months with this church they would have matured in their faith and been able to function well on their own. This is not the case. Paul's two lengthy letters of instruction to this church reveal their spiritual immaturity and their ongoing struggle to walk rightly with Jesus. Perhaps Paul spent so much time there simply because he knew how badly they needed it. And based on the content of these letters, we must wonder if they needed even more of his in-person attention.

For each of these two letters, Paul lists a consignatory.

In his first letter, 1 Corinthians, Paul lists Sosthenes as a co-author. His name only appears one other time in the Bible. We learn in Acts 18:17 that Sosthenes is a synagogue leader. We can safely assume that he later follows Jesus and becomes a leader in Jesus's new church there. Because his name appears on this letter, we can speculate that Sosthenes has come to Paul on behalf of the Corinth church with a list of questions or a report on problems. Perhaps he does both. Regardless,

Sosthenes has a role in writing this dispatch to his friends back home.

In his second letter, 2 Corinthians, Paul lists Timothy as a co-author. We know much more about Timothy. He travels with Paul on some of his missionary journeys, spending time in Corinth with Paul (Acts 18:5). Paul later sends Timothy back there (1 Corinthians 4:17). Again, we can speculate that Timothy carries first-hand information back to Paul, which results in his second letter.

These two letters (sometimes called epistles) that Paul wrote to the church in Corinth are his longest missives. This means that we know more about Paul's instructions to this fledgling church than any of the other faith communities he started or visited.

Paul directs the content of his two letters to the Corinthians, addressing questions they have asked him or their struggles that have come to his attention. Unfortunately, we don't know the details of this relevant background; we only know Paul's response.

This may mean these dispatches do not contain universal truths but are specific reactions to a church with issues. This doesn't mean there isn't value in these letters because there is. But we must exercise care to not take Paul's words out of context.

In the next forty chapters we'll strive to do just that. In this Bible-study-style devotional, we'll examine Paul's teachings to the Corinthian church. As we do, let us rightly discern how his instructions to them two thousand years ago best apply to us today. To accomplish this, may we seek Holy Spirit guidance in reading and exploring 1 and 2 Corinthians.

What do you anticipate you might learn from the Corinthians that can inform your faith practices? If you are part of a church, what similarities do you sense between your church and the church in Corinth?

[Discover more about the church of Corinth in Acts 18.]

DAY 1: NO DIVISIONS
1 CORINTHIANS 1:1–17

That all of you agree with one another in what you say and that there be no divisions among you, but that you be perfectly united in mind and thought. (1 Corinthians 1:10)

Paul wants the Corinthians to function as one and to live in unity—of like mind. But this unity isn't just a message for them because Paul also encourages the churches in Ephesus, Philippi, and Colossae to pursue unity with other believers. In the same way, Jesus prayed that we—his future followers—would live as one, just as he and his Father exist as one (John 17:21).

But to our shame, we divide Jesus's church. We live in disharmony. We fight with each other over our traditions and our practices and how we comprehend God.

We spar over worship style, song selection, and a myriad of other things that relate to church practices and our perception of right living. Or to avoid these errors, we simply ignore those with other perspectives, and that's just as bad.

But the world watches us. They judge Jesus through our actions. They test what we say by the things we do. And we often fail their test.

With our words we talk about how Jesus loves everyone, but with our deeds we diminish our brothers and sisters in Christ with a holier-than-thou discord. If we can't love those in the church, how can we hope to love those outside it? We can't.

It's no wonder the world no longer respects the church of Jesus and is quick to dismiss his followers as hypocritical zealots. We brought it upon ourselves with our church splits and tens of thousands of Protestant denominations, resulting from our petty arguments over practices and theology and everything in between.

In the face of a couple of billion Christians, mostly living life contrary to God's will by not getting along with each other, what can you and I do to correct this error?

We can change this one person at a time. Find another Christian who goes to a church radically different from yours (or has dropped out of church) and embrace them as one in Christ.

If you are a mainline Christian, find a charismatic follower of Jesus and get to know him or her. If all your friends are Protestants, go to Mass and make some new friends.

If all the Christians you know look just like you, think like you, and act like you, find another Christian who is not like you. Diversify your Christian relationships to expand your understanding of what following Jesus truly looks like.

In Jesus, we are the same. It's time we embrace one another. The world is watching us to discover what we do. Instead of seeing our selfishness and sins, may they see Jesus instead.

What can we do to better live in unity with other Christians? What action can we take today?

[Discover more about unity through Jesus in Ephesians 4:3 and Philippians 4:2–3.]

DIG DEEPER: THE DANGERS OF FOLLOWING CHRISTIAN CELEBRITIES

One of you says, "I follow Paul"; another, "I follow Apollos"; another, "I follow Cephas"; still another, "I follow Christ. (1 Corinthians 1:12)

The Christians living in the city of Corinth suffer from an unwise celebration of its leaders (1 Corinthians 1:11–13). They exalt the missionaries who stop by—Paul, Apollos, and Cephas—following them with great zeal (1 Corinthians 3:4–5). They argue over who's the best. In doing so, they divide Jesus and his church, elevating leaders and removing the focus from their Savior who died for them.

Just as it happened 2,000 years ago, it still

happens today. Christians gush with praise over well-known teachers. This adoration of church leaders approaches the level of hero worship. The risk is that the fame of these superstars threatens to supersede Jesus.

Many of these Christian celebrities are featured in books, or they pen their own. There's nothing wrong with this, but what is wrong is following their words with more zeal than believing what the Bible says or following God as revealed in Scripture.

With ungodly fervor, we elevate these cherished leaders, hoisting them to lofty expectations that no one can maintain. Our unbridled admiration only increases their risk of failure and the likelihood of our profound disappointment when they stumble.

It's sad when it happens, and we won't need to wait long before another prominent Christian leader falls from his pedestal. Yes, it's usually men. It may be infidelity, drug abuse, misappropriation of funds, or improper treatment of women. Make no mistake that their moral failings are the sole cause, but our unrestrained, unexamined admiration makes it easier for this to occur.

While the Bible celebrates our faith's heroes, such as in Hebrews 11, it does so posthumously. They've set their record. We know their strengths and their weaknesses. We esteem them, celebrating what is good and guarding against what is not. They can no longer disappoint us by their human failings.

Christian celebrity is dangerous, both for our leaders and for us not putting Jesus first in our lives. May we not fall victim to it. May we instead keep our focus on Jesus. We need to follow him and no one else.

Which spiritual teachers have we put on a pedestal? What must we do to keep our focus on Jesus and not let Christian celebrity get in the way?

[Discover more about putting Jesus first in Matthew 6:33 and Colossians 3:17. Read about putting God first in Exodus 20:3 and Matthew 22:37–40.]

DAY 2: FOOLISHNESS AND WISDOM
1 CORINTHIANS 1:18–2:5

For the foolishness of God is wiser than human wisdom, and the weakness of God is stronger than human strength.
(1 Corinthians 1:25)

Jesus doesn't make sense to most people. They need him, but they don't realize it. They're dying, but they don't see how Christ's sacrificial death on the cross can save them. It's foolishness to them. They think they need to do something to earn their salvation or that being mostly good, most of the time, is enough. God's grace is a free, no-strings-attached gift that escapes their comprehension.

Therefore, they dismiss the good news about Jesus because they don't understand it; they can't. But to those of us on the inside—those who follow Jesus—his death (and resurrection) represents the glory and power of God (1 Corinthians 1:18).

When most not-yet-believers of Jesus consider him, they do so with their mind. It's hard—even impossible—for their intellect to grasp what he says, so they dismiss his message as mere foolishness. They then pronounce that only the ignorant would embrace such nonsense. Without the convicting power of God's Holy Spirit, we would all remain mired in this same perception that following Jesus as our Savior makes no sense. It's utter foolishness.

Yet God renders our worldly wisdom as mere foolishness. Paul explains that every aspect of God, including the parts people may perceive as foolish, far surpass the wisest person. And even at his weakest—such as when he died on the cross—he exceeds the strongest person.

Though God wants us to tell others about Jesus —which should be our natural inclination as his disciples—he never told us to make converts. Instead, he told us to go into the world and make disciples. But how can we make disciples of people who haven't yet believed in Jesus and don't yet follow him because his message is foolishness to them?

Fortunately, this transition from nonbeliever to believer falls to the convicting power of the Holy Spirit. Because Jesus's good news seems like foolishness to the world, we will never talk them into following him. We can't argue anyone into the kingdom of God.

But this isn't an excuse to remain silent. Our words—and our actions—can point people to Jesus. Then the Holy Spirit will go to work, turning what seems foolish to them into an understanding that Jesus is the answer to their pain, a solution to their problems. What they once perceived as foolishness in their mind becomes the wisdom of God in their heart.

Do we attempt to understand Jesus with our intellect? Until the good news of Jesus moves from our head to our heart, we will never accept him, follow him, or be his disciple.

Is Jesus in our head or does he live in our heart? Who can we tell about him?

[Discover more about following Jesus in Matthew 4:19, Mark 10:21, Luke 9:23, and John 10:27.]

DAY 3: THE MIND OF CHRIST
1 CORINTHIANS 2:6–16

We have the mind of Christ. (1 Corinthians 2:16)

Paul continues writing about foolishness and wisdom in what will later become the second chapter of his letter. After sharing additional insights about the subject, he states that those who are spiritual can determine all things, surpassing human judgment. He cites Isaiah, who asks the rhetorical question, who can understand God? (Isaiah 40:13).

Paul concludes this passage by reminding the people that we—he, the Corinthians, and by extension, us today—have the mind of Christ. How amazing is that? What a remarkable truth this is for us to possess the same knowledge as Jesus.

But what does it mean to have the mind of Christ?

This phrase doesn't appear anywhere else in the Bible, so we can't use other verses to help us understand it. This doesn't imply, however, that we should dismiss this as an inexplicable teaching.

First, when we follow Jesus, we perceive him with greater clarity, spiritually understanding him better than would be possible from our limited human intellect alone. This allows us to realize what's important to him and perceive our reality through his eyes. In doing so, we begin to possess the same mindset as he.

Next, having the mind of Christ establishes a framework from which we can better understand God. This revelation comes through both his written word, the Bible, and his spoken word, the Holy Spirit. These insights allow us to better comprehend God's thoughts, aligning our desires with his—not the other way around.

Third, having the mind of Christ results in a deeper understanding of the supernatural. When we do so, we become a spiritual person, able to

Love Is Patient

make judgments about everything (1 Corinthians 2:15).

Last, when we pray with the mind of Christ, we can begin to do so from his perspective. In this way, we cease making superficial requests that address temporal, self-centered desires. Instead, we can replace them with God-centered requests to advance his kingdom and accomplish his will here on earth. In this way, we reform our prayers and inform our outlook from a spiritual, God-aligned perspective.

These outcomes are all ours when we have the mind of Christ. As Jesus's followers we inherently possess this ability, even though we may not realize it. Yet at the same time, having the mind of Christ is a skill we should exercise and seek to develop.

Do we believe we have the mind of Christ? How should this realization inform what we say and do?

[Discover more about having the mind of Christ in Philippians 2:5–8.]

DAY 4: BABY CHRISTIANS
1 CORINTHIANS 3:1–23

I could not address you as people who live by the Spirit but as people who are still worldly—mere infants in Christ.
(1 Corinthians 3:1)

Paul reprimands the church in Corinth for many things. He points out that they envy one another and argue a lot. There is jealousy and quarreling in their church family. They're infants in their faith, behaving like baby Christians.

The people in the Corinthian church want what others have. Although jealousy often relates to money, possessions, or prestige, we can also envy the faith of others, their spiritual journey, and even their intimacy with God. Though wanting these things seems spiritual, wrong motives make their pursuit just as bad. Jealousy is jealousy, regardless of what we long for.

We also see that the Corinthian church abounds with quarrels. They disagree and fight with words. Today, it seems no church is immune to arguing, yet Paul decries it as wrong. Don't do it.

Jealousy and quarreling are worldly traits. They are not godly, but carnal. By allowing these conditions to persist, we prove we are mere humans (1 Corinthians 3:3).

By saying mere humans, Paul implies another way, a higher ground we can take. We don't need to be merely human; we *shouldn't* be merely human.

Through Jesus and the power of his Holy Spirit, we can rise above being mere humans. We can become more than human—superhuman, if you will—not in physical strength but in spiritual might.

As followers of Jesus, being merely human is who we were, but our future is a superhuman spirituality. Are we willing to pursue it?

How do we do this?

We must move from worldly infancy to spiritual maturity. We must stop being infants in Christ.

Too many people in today's church are baby Christians. There's nothing wrong with being new

Love Is Patient

in our faith and needing to receive spiritual milk or be spoon-fed basic nutrients. What's wrong is when we persist in this mode, remaining baby Christians for years, decades, or even our entire life.

God has a better way. He wants us to grow up and learn to feed ourselves. I'm moving in that direction, and I pray you are too.

As a benchmark, ask yourself why you go to church (assuming that you do). Many people will say they go to be fed. They want their minister to provide enough spiritual sustenance on Sunday morning to sustain them throughout the week so they can return seven days later and repeat the experience.

At the risk of causing offense, let me suggest that people who go to church to be fed are baby Christians, mere infants in their faith. I challenge you to pursue a better path, one where we feed ourselves and don't rely on someone else for our supernatural nourishment.

Read and study God's Word. Devote yourself to prayer as you start your day, end your day, and move through your day. But you don't need to do this alone. Invest in other like-minded sojourners and let them invest in you. Feed yourself, and feed one another, not expecting your pastor to do for you each Sunday what Paul says we should do for ourselves.

Honestly ask yourself—or better yet, ask God—if you are a baby Christian. If the answer is yes, seek God to discover how you can learn to feed yourself and grow in your faith.

What do we need to do to move from being an infant in Christ to a spiritually mature follower of Jesus? What can we do today to feed ourselves?

[Discover more about being a baby Christian in Ephesians 4:14–15 and Hebrews 5:12–14.]

DAY 5: WORTHY OF IMITATION
1 CORINTHIANS 4:1–21

Therefore I urge you to imitate me. (1 Corinthians 4:16)

As we read the four biographies of Jesus—by Matthew, Mark, Luke, and John—we see that Jesus offers various instructions to the people who want to align themselves with him. Each instruction seems tailored to the person he speaks to, but the phrase he says most often—implying that it applies to most people—is "repent and follow me" or even more simply, "follow me."

I like that. I identify with that. That's why I often call myself a follower of Jesus—because I am. As his follower, I try to do what he does. I want to be like him. He is worthy of emulation. As a disciple of Jesus, I strive to imitate him. That's a worthy and wise pursuit.

You'd think Paul would say the same thing, but he doesn't. Instead, he urges the people in Corinth to imitate *him*. What audacity. I would never suggest anyone imitate me, for I know I will fall short and not be a worthy example. Yet this isn't what Paul says.

You may have heard the quip that whenever you see the word *therefore* in the Bible, look to see what it's *there for*. This is wise advice. In fact, we should always read Scripture in the context of what comes before and after the verse we're studying.

In this case, what comes before the *therefore* is Paul's justification. He says, "I became your father through the gospel. Therefore I urge you imitate me" (1 Corinthians 4:15–16, NIV).

When we look at this verse in other translations, we often see *imitate* replaced with *follow*, *be like me*, and *follow my example*.

Though we could assume Paul is saying we're to follow him instead of Jesus—God forbid—he later explains what he means. He urges the people to follow his example because he follows Jesus's (1 Corinthians 11:1).

The people in Corinth have never seen Jesus in

Love Is Patient

person. They don't know what his example is because they've never witnessed it. Yet they have seen Paul. They know how Paul conducts himself and lives out his faith. He stands as a tangible reflection of Jesus.

Therefore, when Paul says imitate me, he isn't being arrogant. He's setting himself up as a flesh-and-blood model of Jesus. Through Paul's words and actions, he emulates Jesus, allowing the people in Corinth to have a concrete example to follow.

Though I would never be brave enough to tell someone to imitate me, I'm convicted that I need to do a better job of living a life worthy of imitation. Paul did it. By faith and perseverance, we, too, can become a worthy example to follow.

Who do we imitate? Is our life worthy of emulation?

[Discover more about imitating others in 2 Thessalonians 3:9, Hebrews 6:12, Hebrews 13:7, and 3 John 1:11.]

DAY 6: JUDGE OTHERS OR NOT
1 CORINTHIANS 5:1–13

What business is it of mine to judge those outside the church?
(1 Corinthians 5:12)

In 1 Corinthians, Paul talks a dozen times about judgment. Only the much longer books of Psalms and Ezekiel mention the word *judge* more often.

This theme of judging comes up again when Paul addresses sexual sin within the church, specifically incest—a topic I'm loath to mention.

Reading between the lines, we infer some of the people in Corinth think God's grace gives them the freedom to pursue sexual immorality, to live as they wish, while the rest of the church remains quiet on the issue.

Paul's concern is that one poor example will infect others and embolden them to go wild as well. As the saying goes, "one bad apple spoils the whole barrel," though Paul's first-century version says a bit of yeast affects the whole batch.

In this passage, we could assume Paul commands the Corinthian church to ostracize sinners, to shun them, but many other verses in the New Testament commend and even command the opposite approach. (See the verses below in "Discover more.")

Instead, Paul's intent is to focus on professed followers of Jesus who purposefully sin and then celebrate what they're doing as a demonstration of God's love, grace, and mercy. They boast in what they do, and the church boasts in allowing them to do so.

Though Paul expects them to assess the situation and act, he places limits on their role of judging others. This is the more important part of his instruction.

Specifically, Paul says not to worry about those on the outside. God will deal with them. Instead, they need to focus their concern on the people

Love Is Patient

within their group, that self-policing is in order. Paul reminds them that they should judge folks within the church, but they have no business judging people in the world.

Much of today's church has this backward. We delight in pointing a condemning finger at the actions of the world, all the while ignoring the behavior within our own community.

It's no wonder the world thinks the church consists of close-minded, judgmental hypocrites, since we too often prove it by what we say and do. Because of our words and our actions, the world doesn't see the love of Jesus. Instead, we show them mean, hateful judgment.

Though we need to judge those in our church who boast in their sins, we have no business judging others in the world.

Who do we judge? Why? What must we change in our perspective about judging others?

[Discover more about not judging others in Matthew 6:12, Matthew 7:1–3, John 8:7, 1 Corinthians 4:3, and James 2:3–4.]

DIG DEEPER: THE LOST LETTER

I wrote to you in my letter . . . (1 Corinthians 5:9)

The Bible contains two letters that Paul wrote to the church in Corinth. But there is a third one, a dispatch not included in Scripture. Paul references this other letter—which was actually his first one—in 1 Corinthians.

In this initial letter Paul says he told the Corinthians to not associate with sexually immoral people. His words were imprecise, and they misunderstood him, thinking he meant the immoral people in the world. To do that, they would need to remove themselves from society. But if they did, how could they—and we by extension—tell them about Jesus?

Instead, Paul meant those *within* the church, which he clarifies here in 1 Corinthians.

That's all we know about this first letter—the lost letter—that Paul wrote to the Corinthian church. I wish we had it to read and study. It would deepen our understanding of this flawed community and their many issues, informing us today with our many issues.

Yet we don't have this letter. The recipients didn't preserve it for our benefit.

This isn't the only time this happened. Another of Paul's letters disappeared as well and is not found in our Scriptures. This is a letter to the church in Laodicea. Following the naming convention of Paul's other letters, we might have referred to this letter as Laodiceans.

In Paul's letter to the Colossians, he tells them to share their letter with the church in Laodicea and vice versa.

We see that not all the churches preserved Paul's letters. Though these messages could have helped us—and all future generations—we'll never know because we don't have them to read.

What can we do today to encourage future generations on their faith journey?

[Discover more about Paul's other missing letter in Colossians 4:16.]

DAY 7: LITIGIOUS CHRISTIANS
1 CORINTHIANS 6:1–11

The very fact that you have lawsuits among you means you have been completely defeated already. (1 Corinthians 6:5)

I cringe every time I hear a report of Christians not getting along and pursuing legal action. Though this newsworthy rancor sometimes occurs within the context of a denomination meeting or a church setting, it also happens when one group of Christians sues another.

This can be a church suing its denomination, a lawsuit to remove a pastor, or litigious church members contending with each other. Other examples include a Christian businessman suing his Christian partner, lawsuits and countersuits filed over a church split, or suing a church board over the decisions they have made.

Adding fuel to this inferno, reporters share soundbites from the aggrieved parties. Their rhetoric proves to the watching public that Christians are selfish people who act just like everyone else instead of demonstrating a loving contrast to worldly behavior.

What a terrible message this sends about Christianity. Our actions provide the worst possible witness to lost people who need Jesus. My heart grieves each time this occurs. Not only is it bad public relations, even more significant, it's unbiblical.

Paul says that suing over a matter between Christians in a secular court proves that both parties have already lost. No one wins when we expect the world's judges to decide between warring litigants who claim to align with Jesus.

Paul continues by saying that instead of a lawsuit, the better solution is to accept the wrongs of others, to endure cheating without seeking justice in the court of unbelievers.

Jesus taught the same thing. He says that if anyone sues you for your shirt, you should offer them your coat as well (Matthew 5:40). Suffering in

Love Is Patient

silence is more God honoring than litigating in public.

Christians should decide these matters within the church, not outside of it. We see this occur in the book of Acts in the account of how the early church functions.

Peter goes to the Gentiles, and they receive the Holy Spirit. This should be a reason to celebrate: the good news is for everyone, not just the Jews. Yet not everyone sees it this way. Some of the circumcised believers (converts from Judaism) criticize Peter's actions because he's interacting with non-Jews.

Though they could bring their complaints to outside authorities, instead they resolve this internally. Their solution is simple. They let Peter explain himself. Once he does, he eases their concerns, and they praise God (Acts 11:1–18).

Another time, a theological dispute arises after some men teach that circumcision is a prerequisite for salvation. Paul and Barnabas disagree. A debate ensues. To resolve the issue, a delegation goes to the main church in Jerusalem where the church leaders meet to decide the matter. They send letters of their decision to the churches in the area, which the people read and receive with gladness (Acts 15:1–31).

A third example in the book of Acts is about a disagreement between Barnabas and Paul. It grows so intense that they end their missionary partnership. They go their separate ways, each taking on new mentees. They make this decision without involving church leadership. More importantly, they don't try to get others in the church to side with them and oppose the other. This stands as an excellent example of dealing with conflict in a God-honoring way (Acts 15:36–41).

How should we handle conflict and disagreement with others who follow Jesus? What actions should we change to be a better witness to those outside our faith?

[Discover more about conflict in Hebrews 10:32–35.]

DAY 8: GOD'S TEMPLES
1 CORINTHIANS 6:12–20

Do you not know that your bodies are temples of the Holy Spirit, who is in you, whom you have received from God?
(1 Corinthians 6:19)

The temple is an important fixture for the religious rituals of the Jews in Paul's day, but this practice starts back in the Old Testament. It begins with the tabernacle established by Moses as the place where the people go to encounter God and worship him. Later, King Solomon builds the temple to replace the tabernacle. Again, this serves as the centralized place where the people of Israel go to experience God.

They perceive the temple—and the tabernacle

before it—as God's dwelling place on earth. They go to the temple to offer their sacrifices and present their tithes.

Yet when Jesus comes, he changes this. In fact, he changes everything.

When we follow him, we can approach God directly, from anywhere, at any time. We no longer need to go to the temple—or to a church building—to connect with the Almighty. This is because, through Jesus, our bodies have become temples of God's Holy Spirit. He lives in us, not in a building. This means that we take God's temple with us wherever we go.

Today's passage, however, isn't the first time Paul mentions this earth-shattering idea. He's already told the Corinthian church this once, earlier in this same letter. He asks them, perhaps rhetorically, don't you remember you are God's temple? Did you forget God lives in you? (1 Corinthians 3:16).

He now tells them these truths a second time to make sure they comprehend it and don't miss this important reality.

Jesus foreshadows this truth of us being God's temple.

First, when the Jews contend with him, they ask

Love Is Patient

him for a supernatural sign to prove his authority. He says he will destroy this temple and raise it again in three days. They mock him for his audacity, not comprehending that he's talking about his body and not the physical temple in Jerusalem (John 2:18–19). In this rebuilt temple—of Jesus, through Jesus, and in Jesus—we can anticipate he will change the temple, fulfilling the Old Testament Law (Matthew 5:17).

Second, Jesus tells his followers that he will send them the Holy Spirit to help them and be with them forever (Luke 24:49, John 14:16–17, and Acts 1:4–5).

Through Jesus, we see a new temple and receive the Holy Spirit. In this way, we become temples of God's Holy Spirit.

How should the knowledge that we are God's temple change our behavior? How can having the Holy Spirit living in us empower us?

[Discover more about being God's temple in Ephesians 2:19–22.]

DAY 9: SEX, MARRIAGE, AND LIFE
1 CORINTHIANS 7:1–40

Now for the matters you wrote about . . . (1 Corinthians 7:1)

You may recall that the contents of Paul's two letters to the Corinthian church are instructions about problems that have come to his attention or answers to questions they've asked. The opening to this chapter confirms this. Though other parts of Paul's letter may address their questions, we know for certain that this chapter does.

It's easy to imagine that each section or thought in this chapter answers one of their questions. We don't know, however, what those questions are. This makes it challenging to determine how to interpret them and discern how to apply what Paul writes.

Another interesting fact is that several times in this chapter Paul shares his opinion (verses 8, 12, 25, and 40), yet one time he says that the command comes from God (verse 10).

A second interesting tidbit is Paul's perception that their time remaining on earth is short (1 Corinthians 7:29), a sentiment he shares in at least one of his other letters (Philippians 4:5). With hindsight, we now see—some 2,000 years later—that the end was not as close as Paul thought. Yet this is the context of his statements.

This issue of making assumptions about the future timeline reminds us of Jeremiah's instructions to the exiles in Babylon. He urges them to push aside their short-term outlook. He tells them to settle down, build houses, plant gardens, get married, have children, and see that their children marry. He wants them to have an impact where they are, even if it's not where they want to be (Jeremiah 29:5–7).

Though the people Jeremiah addressed only needed to wait seventy years to go home, we've been waiting much longer, and it's reasonable to expect we'll continue waiting even more. After all,

Love Is Patient

most every generation since Jesus assumed that time was short. Yet we're still here.

As we read Paul's opinions in this chapter (contrasted to God's commands), we must keep the apostle's short-term context in mind.

First, Paul urges abstinence and later writes that he wishes all would be like him: single and celibate. Yet he also admits that marriage and sex are the best solution for those who struggle with temptation (see 1 Corinthians 10:13). Though he doesn't mention other aspects of marriage, such as love, procreation, and raising children, remember that Paul is a bachelor.

He continues by advising that the unmarried stay unmarried and the married remain married, even if one spouse is not a believer. (With a church full of converts, it's reasonable to assume that many are married to unbelievers.)

In short, he tells them to remain in whatever state they're in, be it single or married, circumcised or not, and slave or free. This makes sense if we believe our remaining days on earth are short.

Since we don't know when time will end, we should strive to impact our world, in the best way possible, for the rest of our lives. And changing our circumstance may provide the opportunity to better advance God's kingdom. This might include finding a new job, getting married, or returning to school. The choice is ours.

Do we have a long-term perspective or think the end is near? How do we best live a life aligned with that outlook? What needs to change?

[Discover more about what Jesus says about the end of this age in Matthew 24:36–39, Mark 13:32–37, and Luke 17:26–35.]

DAY 10: FREEDOM IN JESUS
1 CORINTHIANS 8:1–13

Be careful, however, that the exercise of your rights does not become a stumbling block to the weak. (1 Corinthians 8:9)

The Old Testament of the Bible is about rules, requirements, and regulations. Lots of them. Many Christians today persist in following rules, both those they find in Old Testament Scripture and what they or other people have made up. They're legalistic. As a result, their faith comes with a bunch of rules to follow. This includes activities to do and activities to avoid.

They, like their Old Testament counterparts, also live with the constant pain of failure. They can't fully obey every element of God's Old

Testament laws or their modern-day extensions of them. One tiny slipup, one time, and they fail in totality (James 2:10).

Fortunately, Jesus comes to fulfill the Old Testament law (Matthew 5:17). He offers us a better way: to follow him (Luke 9:23). Instead of rules that we can't fully follow and the judgment our failure demands, Jesus offers us grace and mercy. He extends love instead of exacting punishment.

By removing the burden of rule follower, which always ends with us becoming a rule breaker, we instead have freedom in Jesus. This is not freedom to sin but the freedom to fully live (Romans 6:1–2).

In Paul's letters, we see that the church in Corinth struggles with this rules-versus-freedom issue. For them it relates to food sacrificed to idols, to false gods.

Some see this as an affront to their faith, as if eating sacrificed meat aligns them with the idol that received a sacrifice. Just as we celebrate Communion to remember Jesus, I wonder if some in the Corinthian church worry that eating the meat of a sacrificed animal amounts to idol worship.

Others, however, carry no concern about eating the meat offered to idols. They know the true God through Jesus and they dismiss the idol as a pretend god that means nothing. To them it's a nonissue.

When guided by their conscience, both perspectives are correct.

The person who abstains from eating idol-sacrificed meat does so in reverence to God. Yet the person who eats that same meat does so out of the knowledge that it carries no spiritual significance and is merely a practical option to feed themselves.

The problem occurs when people who refrain from eating animal-sacrificed meat see those on the other side of this debate eating it without reservation. The first group follows the example of the second, despite their conscience gnawing in their gut and telling them it's wrong.

Eating meat sacrificed to idols, however, isn't a factor for us today. So we can skip 1 Corinthians 8, right? No.

We must seek ways to apply this principle to the reality in our world, looking for activities we should stop doing for the sake of how it might affect someone else's faith. It's up to each of us to decide how to apply this to our practices and better protect the consciences of other Jesus followers.

Remember, just because we have the freedom to do something doesn't mean we should.

What do we do that might offend other followers of Jesus and cause them to stumble? How should we follow our conscience and not let the example of other Christians affect our sense of what's right for us?

[Discover what else Paul says about this subject in 1 Corinthians 10:23–33. Read more about sin, right living, death, freedom, and eternal life in Romans 6.]

DAY 11: RUN TO WIN
1 CORINTHIANS 9:1–27

I have become all things to all people so that by all possible means I might save some. (1 Corinthians 9:22)

Paul builds on this idea of freedom by sharing how he applies it to his own life. Though he is free through Jesus and a slave to none, he willingly gives up his freedom to become, in effect, a slave to everyone. The goal is not needless suffering or self-imposed mortification but winning as many as possible to follow Jesus.

For the Jews who obey the law, Paul adheres to it with great zeal. He does this so that he will not cause offense, will get their attention, and can win them to the cause of Christ.

For everyone else, the Gentiles, Paul becomes like them—not following Jewish traditions—so that he might win them too. When he is with those who struggle with their faith, he becomes like they are so he can better connect with them and tell them about Jesus's good news.

He summarizes his strategy as becoming all things to all people so that he can have every opportunity possible to save *some* of them.

It's a lofty approach and worthy of emulation.

Paul equates his efforts to save souls—winning as many as possible—to running a race. He runs with intention. He runs to win, to win souls. So should we.

This idea of pressing onward to win a prize is also a call to finish strong. We should strive to move forward in life, to pursue Jesus and advance his kingdom until our last day on earth. Though we may retire from work, we should never retire from Jesus.

The goal is not to slide into heaven by the smallest of margins, but to enter triumphantly because we won our race.

Some people decide to follow Jesus and think they're all set, that they don't need to do anything more to hold on to him. They correctly assume

Love Is Patient

they're in but wrongly conclude they can do whatever they want the rest of their life, because as far as eternity is concerned, their actions here don't matter.

But this way of thinking is flawed.

Jesus doesn't want us to coast our way into heaven. Instead, we should strive, like Paul, to bring as many people with us as we can. We should pursue our faith as though it is the only thing that matters, because it is.

What are we doing to save as many as possible? Are we running our race hard to the very end?

[Discover more about Paul's desire to finish (win) his race in Acts 20:24, Philippians 3:14, and 2 Timothy 4:7.]

DAY 12: THE TEMPTATION TO SIN
1 CORINTHIANS 10:1–13

When you are tempted, he will also provide a way out so that you can endure it. (1 Corinthians 10:13)

The first sin recorded in the Bible occurs when Adam and Eve eat fruit from the forbidden tree. The future of humanity changes forever, and God kicks them out of the garden. The second sin recorded in the Bible is Cain killing his brother Abel. Springing out of jealousy, the first murder occurs.

But before Cain prematurely ends Abel's life, God issues him a warning. It's a concise three-point teaching about sin (Genesis 4:7). Though issued to

Cain and written about him, it equally applies to us today.

First, sin is crouching at our door. The word *crouch* reminds us of a cat getting ready to pounce on its prey. The situation is ominous.

Next, sin desires to have us. Once the cat leaps for its quarry, there's little doubt over the outcome. Sin is getting ready to leap and destroy us. There's little we can do—or is there?

Third, we must control it. Repelling the temptation to sin is much easier to accomplish beforehand rather than when we're struggling in the middle of it. When temptation crouches, the potential for sin is there, but it's not actual sin. It's temptation (see 1 Corinthians 10:13). The outcome is up to us.

From Scripture, we know what to do with temptation and the devil who suggests it. We are to resist the wrong thought and our enemy will scurry away (James 4:7).

But how do we resist the temptation to sin?

I suspect the church in Corinth asks Paul the same question. He gives them a succinct teaching on the subject to provide them—and us—a godly perspective about temptation. This should encourage us and instruct us how to best respond.

Love Is Patient

Preparing to deal with temptation now provides a path to avoid a bigger problem later.

First, Paul tells the Corinthians that their temptation to do wrong isn't unique to them. It's a common fight for all. Others have struggled with the same issues in the past. This means other people know of the battle and can help us better deal with ours. This is why an alcoholic in the AA program has a sponsor. The sponsor has struggled with that same temptation to drink and can support their charge when the temptation to imbibe confronts them.

Second, God limits the temptation to what we can handle. This doesn't mean he's the source of our wayward desire. Rather, he restricts the enemy's power to afflict us. Because God confines the scope of temptation, this means the Almighty is setting us up to succeed—not fail. How encouraging.

Third, and most comforting, is that God will provide a way out. We can ask him to enable us to see this alternate path, give us the will to take it, and provide the strength to persevere.

Then we can withstand the temptation, just as he promised.

In our struggle with temptation—whatever it may be—how can we apply Paul's teaching so we can resist it? In what ways might God provide a way out?

[Discover more about temptation in Galatians 6:1, Hebrews 2:18, Hebrews 4:15, and James 1:13–14.]

DAY 13: FLEE FROM IDOLATRY
1 CORINTHIANS 10:14–22

Therefore, my dear friends, flee from idolatry.
(1 Corinthians 10:14)

Which book in the New Testament talks most about idols and idolatry? First Corinthians, of course. We've already discussed meat sacrificed to idols in Chapter 10, "Freedom in Jesus," and we'll address more in Chapter 16, "An Unworthy Manner" and Chapter 33, "Yoked with Unbelievers."

For the Corinthian church, the issue of idolatry comes up in relation to eating the meat of animals sacrificed to these false gods. Worshiping idols is a pagan practice, and it has no place in Jesus's church. Some people in the church have a problem eating this meat, while others don't see it as an issue.

Paul warns the church in Corinth against giving their attention to idols and idol worship. He contrasts these pagan feasts with Communion, noting that they shouldn't celebrate both idols and God. Doing so insults their Lord.

The literal practice of idol worship doesn't connect with most people today. Yet the principle most definitely applies, and we should take it more seriously.

The dictionary says idolatry is the worship of idols. We understand this. A secondary definition, however, is more insightful. It explains that idolatry is excessive devotion to something.

Excessiveness is a sin that many in our modern society excel in.

First, many people—especially men—have an excessive devotion to their work. Though employment is essential to earn money to support our families, it's critical to place limits on how much of our time and attention our jobs receive. Placing too high of a priority on our vocation is a modern-day form of idol worship.

Next is possessions. We live in a materialistic society that always seeks more. We buy items, not because we need them, but because we want them. We crave owning something newer, something bigger, something better. It's sometimes called "keeping up with the Joneses," this yearning to have everything our neighbors have. When newer, bigger, and better preoccupies our desires and directs our purchases, we've developed an excessive devotion to materialism, buying things we want but don't need.

A special category of possessions is money. Too many people view their annual income and the size of their bank account as a measure of success. Regardless of how large the number, they strive to make it greater, pursuing an insatiable drive to maximize their income and amass more wealth. Though we need money to live, we shouldn't live for money.

What about hobbies? A hobby is an activity outside of work pursued primarily for pleasure or self-fulfillment. Hobbies kept in balance provide personal benefit, yet hobbies pursued with excessive devotion become our idol and distract us from God. Instead of dismissing hobbies as not God honoring, however, seek ways to use your natural passions and interests for God's glory or to advance his kingdom.

Next, closely related to hobbies, are leisure and entertainment. Again, we need to relax from the day-to-day pace of normal living. This is good and needed for our mental well-being. If we're not careful, however, how we fill our discretionary time can expand to an out-of-balance lifestyle. Seek areas of recreation that draw you to God and don't distract you from him.

Last, let's talk about family. Mentioning family may seem out of place in this discussion. Yet I've seen parents with a child-first focus elevate family to a level that supersedes all else, including the pursuit of God and faith. Families, sadly, can receive an excessive devotion that approaches idolatry.

Though the actual physical act of bowing down to idols and worship is seldom an issue in today's world, the figurative worship of modern idols that receive our excessive devotion stands as an all-too-present threat that we must be careful to avoid.

As Paul says, we must flee from idolatry—in all its forms. This includes an unwarranted preoccupation with work, possessions, money, hobbies, leisure activities, and family.

When we put God first, other things fall into their rightful place.

What have we given our excessive devotion to? What must we do to make God our priority in everything?

[Discover more about idolatry in Galatians 5:19–21, Colossians 3:5, and 1 Peter 4:3.]

DIG DEEPER: JUDGE

Judge for yourselves what I say. (1 Corinthians 10:15)

In Chapter 6, "Judge Others or Not," we mentioned that the word *judge* occurs twelve times in 1 Corinthians, more often than any other book in the New Testament. Here's a list of those passages, some of which we've covered elsewhere, along with a summary:

- 1 Corinthians 4:3, Paul doesn't judge himself.
- 1 Corinthians 4:4, Paul leaves it to God to judge him.

- 1 Corinthians 4:5, withhold judgment until Jesus returns.
- 1 Corinthians 5:12, don't judge those outside the church.
- 1 Corinthians 5:13, expel the wicked from your church community.
- 1 Corinthians 6:2, as Jesus's followers, we will later judge the world.
- 1 Corinthians 6:3, we will also judge angels.
- 1 Corinthians 6:5, we should judge our own disputes and not rely on outsiders.
- 1 Corinthians 10:15, we should judge for ourselves what Paul writes.
- 1 Corinthians 10:29, don't let others judge our freedom in Jesus.
- 1 Corinthians 11:13, judge this issue for yourselves.
- 1 Corinthians 11:32, receive God's judgment as discipline.

With this as a framework for further study, examine each verse. As you do, consider the passage's surrounding text to understand its context. Doing so will enable you to better comprehend the teaching and discern how to apply it.

In what ways do Paul's instructions to the Corinthians about judging apply today? In what ways should we be more careful in how we judge?

[Discover more about judging others in Matthew 7:1–2, Luke 6:37, Romans 14:10, Colossians 2:16, and James 2:3–4.]

DAY 14: PUT OTHERS FIRST
1 CORINTHIANS 10:23–11:1

No one should seek their own good, but the good of others.
(1 Corinthians 10:24)

Many people in developed countries subsist in a narcissistic, self-centered existence. We put ourselves first and care only about what's in our best interest. Too many people live their life with the attitude that "it's all about me." In doing so, they miss so much.

Let me share a secret: It's not all about you.

Life should be about everyone else. When we put others first, we benefit them, glorify God, and enrich ourselves.

Paul reminds the church in Corinth about this.

He tells them to not seek what's in their own best interest but to instead pursue what's in the best interest of others.

This, however, requires balance. For example, if an oxygen mask drops while on an airplane, you should put yours on first and then help your seatmate. If you don't, you might pass out before you can help others in need. Then you both suffer.

In another instance, I once read of a family so intent on feeding their hungry neighbors that some of them starved to death in the process.

Self-preservation is crucial, but beyond that, we should put others first. The Bible says to. What does this look like? It's up for each of us to decide.

It could be as simple as stepping aside to let someone get in line ahead of us. It might be to give someone a ride, even though it would make us late.

What if helping someone would cause us to miss the beginning of a church service? Or even miss it completely? The thought horrifies many, but I suspect it would delight God, shining as an even better act of worship than singing about him during a church service.

How about giving up a seat on the bus and standing?

Love Is Patient

It could mean mowing our neighbor's lawn even though ours needs more attention.

Should we take the last piece of pizza or let someone else enjoy it?

What about walking so someone else can drive our car? Even more bold, how about giving someone our car because he or she needs it more?

We can do many things to seek the good of others, so many that it might overwhelm us. But instead of letting the number of options paralyze us into inaction, pick one thing and then do it.

Doing good for others is the right thing. We do this for them, and we do this for God's glory.

What's one thing we should start doing to put someone else first? How can we do all things for the glory of God?

[Discover more about Paul's teaching on putting others first in Romans 15:1–3 and Philippians 2:3–4.]

DAY 15: INTERDEPENDENT
1 CORINTHIANS 11:2–16

In the Lord woman is not independent of man, nor is man independent of woman. (1 Corinthians 11:11)

The next section in Paul's letter is one that many people want to skim or even skip. Others stumble over it. It's about women and their hair, but that's not the point.

Bookending this passage is Paul's discussion about what's proper when people—men and women—pray and prophesy, presumably at a church meeting. He may be giving commands to follow, but these come across as bordering on misogynistic, not to mention confusing, especially given our perspective in today's society.

A more reasonable understanding, however, is that Paul is connecting the Corinthian church's practices with the societal conventions of their day. He wants them to reform what they're doing and adopt a more appropriate process.

We're better off focusing on the verses that occur in the middle of this passage. They're easy to miss, given what precedes and follows them, but this is the heart of the text, the meat of the sandwich.

After providing a lengthy introduction to his topic, Paul marks a transition by saying "nevertheless." It's as if he diminishes what he's just said to focus on something more critical to the discussion. He next writes that as followers of Jesus (that is, the Lord), men aren't independent of women and women aren't independent of men. The two genders function as interdependent.

As the first woman (Eve) came from a man (Adam), all men from then on have come from women. We live interdependently with each other, for one can't exist without the other. And both come from God (1 Corinthians 11:11–12). God created us, both male and female, in his own image (Genesis 1:27).

What Paul writes next is even more interesting. He instructs the church in Corinth to judge for themselves: is it proper for women to pray with their heads uncovered?

This may be a rhetorical question, where the answer is self-evident to his audience. But from today's perspective, the answer is anything but obvious. We could also take Paul's instruction to judge for themselves as a literal directive, as in "the decision is up to you."

This is the passage's key takeaway. Though we could debate the issue and build a doctrine around head coverings and hair length, we're better off avoiding the quagmire and leaving the decision up to each person, both male and female, as created in God's image.

How can the knowledge that men and women are not independent alter our gender perspectives? What practices or attitudes should we change for our church gatherings?

[Discover more on God's view of gender in Matthew 19:4, Mark 10:6, and Galatians 3:28.]

DAY 16: AN UNWORTHY MANNER
1 CORINTHIANS 11:17–34

For those who eat and drink without discerning the body of Christ eat and drink judgment on themselves.
(1 Corinthians 11:29)

Taking Communion (the Eucharist) today is usually a solemn affair, steeped with reverence and ritual. There's nothing wrong with this, but shouldn't the Lord's Supper be a celebration?

What's the purpose of Communion? It's something we do to remember what Jesus did for us. He died. More importantly, he overcame death by rising from the grave. His victory can be our victory, and it's worthy of a party.

When I take Communion at church I try to focus on the why, but I often struggle. The process distracts me, especially if I'm visiting a new church. I become so fixated on how they practice the Lord's Supper that I forget to focus on why. Though I expect celebrating Communion to produce a highly spiritual encounter, I'm often disappointed.

Although Paul writes many letters to various churches and individuals, only to the Corinthians does he address the Lord's Supper. We can suspect this is because the church in Corinth struggles with its practice of Holy Communion. This may be one question they ask Paul, or maybe someone has alerted him to their failure to observe the Lord's Supper in a God-honoring remembrance of Jesus.

Regardless, Paul writes to them, seeking to reorient their procedure to focus on Jesus and not themselves.

The first of two relevant passages in this letter provides general instructions relating to food and drink, as well as idol worship and freedom through Jesus. These verses connect to the practice of Communion (1 Corinthians 10:14–33).

The second passage with verses about Communion is in the next chapter. It specifically

Love Is Patient

addresses how the Corinthian church abuses this sacrament (1 Corinthians 11:17–34).

Paul reminds them what Jesus taught his disciples about this practice. It helps keep them, and us, on track—or gets us back on track.

Tucked in the middle of this passage is a convicting verse warning about taking Communion unworthily. This gives any believer pause, for no one wants to commit this sin—even if we're unsure of what it refers to.

To understand what Paul means, we must consider the abuses Paul details. Specifically, the Corinthian church's practice of Communion diverges from Jesus's intent so much that Paul deems it does more harm than good. To correct this, they should examine themselves to make sure they aren't part of the problem that Paul details.

Paul wants them to guard against getting drunk during their celebration of the Lord's Supper. He also urges them to be sure everyone takes part together, with each person having enough to eat and no one leaving hungry. Mostly he wants them to keep their focus on Jesus and not the food and drink.

These are the things Paul tells the Corinthian

church to examine. If this applies to us, we, too, should embark on some self-examination.

Though some churches today encourage attendees to examine themselves before partaking in the Lord's Supper, they miss the context of this passage. They wrongly take an introspective look at their relationship with God (which is a wise move in other situations) instead of focusing on their attitude and relationship with the other people taking Communion with them.

What must we change to make Communion a more meaningful spiritual experience? How might our practice of the Lord's Supper do more harm than good?

[Discover more about the practice of communion in Matthew 26:17–30, Mark 14:12–26, and Luke 22:7–23.]

DAY 17: THIRTEEN SPIRITUAL GIFTS
1 CORINTHIANS 12:1–11

Now about the gifts of the Spirit, brothers and sisters, I do not want you to be uninformed. (1 Corinthians 12:1)

In his first letter to the church in Corinth, Paul talks a lot about the gifts of the Spirit, which we commonly call spiritual gifts. Here's what he says.

First, these gifts come from the Holy Spirit, who supernaturally endows us with special abilities. This includes various functions, but they're all the result of God at work in us and through us.

Next, these gifts are for our common good as Jesus's church. These presents that God gives us are to benefit others, not ourselves. They help our church community, or they serve others outside the church. Sometimes they do both. When used properly, our gifts of the Spirit advance the kingdom of God, for his glory.

Third, God doesn't equip us all with the same abilities. He gives each of us the spiritual gift or gifts needed to accomplish his divine purpose. Though we may wish to have the same ability as someone else, we would be wrong to desire that person's spiritual gift or begrudge them for it.

Fourth, God gives them—and us—the spiritual gift he does because he is sovereign (a good sovereign), able to do whatever he wishes.

Lastly, the church comprises one body made up of various interconnected parts, represented by the spiritual gifts he provides to us. (We'll talk about this more in the next chapter.)

Here are thirteen spiritual gifts that Paul mentions (1 Corinthians 12:8–10). This list isn't comprehensive, but it's a terrific start:

1. **Wisdom**: the ability to apply spiritual truth to meet specific needs or situations.
2. **Knowledge**: provide truth by revealing critical information, biblical understanding, or supernatural insight.

Love Is Patient

(Whereas wisdom is the ability to apply commonly known truth, knowledge is the ability to receive and share with others what is unknown.)

3. **Faith**: the confidence that God will provide, protect, and answer prayers.
4. **Healing**: the ability to pray, touch, or speak words to produce spiritual, physical, or emotional healing.
5. **Miracles**: show God's power through supernatural action.
6. **Prophecy**: guide others by speaking truth to cause correction or repentance.
7. **Discernment**: the ability to distinguish between truth and error, fact and fiction.
8. **Tongues**: talk in a language unknown to the speaker for prayer, worship, or the benefit of others.
9. **Interpretation**: tell others what someone said in tongues.

A bit later, Paul adds additional items to the list (1 Corinthians 12:28). Though he doesn't specifically call them gifts, God does assign them. In this passage, Paul repeats miracles, healing, and speaking in tongues. But he also includes four more possibilities:

1. **Apostleship**: oversee and lead a ministry or missionary effort.
2. **Teaching**: understand and explain biblical truth to help others apply it to their lives and grow in faith.
3. **Helps (Service)**: assist a ministry or person to meet needs and accomplish objectives.
4. **Administration**: organize and execute ministry goals.

What spiritual gifts has the Holy Spirit given to you? How can we more fully honor God by using the gifts he's provided to us for his church's benefit?

[Discover more about the gifts of the Spirit in Romans 12:6–8 and Ephesians 4:11. See other spiritual gifts in Exodus 31:3, 1 Corinthians 7:7, and 1 Peter 4:9–10.]

DAY 18: ONE BODY UNITED
1 CORINTHIANS 12:12–31

For we were all baptized by one Spirit so as to form one body —whether Jews or Gentiles, slave or free. (1 Corinthians 12:13)

Paul gives the Corinthians an illustration to help them understand why God allocates spiritual gifts the way he does. Think of a body with its various parts: a head, ears, eyes, hands, feet, and so forth.

A person with two heads would exist in perpetual conflict with itself. Or consider a head with many eyes and no ears. Though it could see many things, it would hear nothing. What about many feet and no hands? Though the individual could move around, there's little it could accomplish once it arrived.

One part of our body can't tell another part it's not needed. Each part has a purpose, and without it we would cease to be whole. Without one or more of our major organs, we would struggle to function as God intended. Also, some aspects of our body receive much honor, while we cover other areas and let them function in the background, even though those functions are essential.

We have one body with many organs.

The same is true with the church—that is, the *body* of Christ. For the church body to function as it should, all parts must be present and work together, each doing what God designed it to do. Just as a human being has diversity in its components, so does Jesus's church. Through a diversity of people with various gifts of the Spirit, our church can become a unified whole.

The church is one body, living in unity—or at least it should be. But it has many parts (members). Each person functions for the well-being of the body, as God enables them to do so with their gifts of the Spirit.

Just as Jesus's church has people with different

spiritual gifts, it also enjoys a diversity of people with different physical attributes. In both ways, we are one body.

Paul tells the church in Corinth there's no difference between being Jewish or Greek, slave or free. In his letter to the church in Colossae Paul expands this list to include circumcised, uncircumcised, barbarian, and uncivilized. And to the church in Galatia, he adds male and female.

Think about this. Contemplate the ramifications. Paul tells us to break down all divisions over ethnicity, social status, gender, and religious practices.

He wants us to function as one and live in unity. In the same way, Jesus wants us to live as one, just as he and his Father exist as one.

Today we need to apply this essential need for unity to the church Jesus started. We must add that when we follow Jesus, there's no difference between being Orthodox, Catholic, or Protestant; Mainline, Evangelical, or Charismatic.

Then we will be truly united to form one body.

How can we live out Paul's command to break down our divisions? What is the biggest obstacle to us living in the unity Jesus prayed for? What steps can we take to bring about unity in Jesus?

[Discover more about being one body united in Jesus in John 17:21, Galatians 3:28, and Colossians 3:11.]

DAY 19: LOVE IS PATIENT
1 CORINTHIANS 13:1–10

Love is patient, love is kind. It does not envy, it does not boast, it is not proud. (1 Corinthians 13:4)

How many times do you say *love* each day? Don't answer too quickly. Our world has a skewed understanding of love. Most of us misuse it—often.

Consider some of these common uses of the word love:

- I love to watch movies.
- I love that shirt.
- I love pizza.
- I love that dog.

- I love that car.
- I love to read the Bible.
- I love my family.
- I love you.
- I love God.

These are all phrases I've used. I suspect you've said similar things too.

But they convey different meanings of the word *love*, ranging from preference to passion. What is love? Our society treats love as an emotion, but let's consider love as an attitude that prompts unselfish action.

Though we may use the word *love* to show our preference or as an intensifier to amplify our words, we're wrong to do so. We can't love an object or an activity. We can't even love an animal, not really. But we can love God and the people he created.

Even then, we must be careful how we use the word *love*. The next time you think about saying *love*, pause before you speak and consider if it's the right situation.

To love others, Paul gives the Corinthian church some helpful instructions on how to do this correctly, on how to love others in a God-honoring

Love Is Patient

way. By following these verses, we can love others according to Scripture.

Paul's list of love's attributes helps inform our understanding. He writes that love is:

- patient
- kind
- not envious
- not boastful
- not proud
- not rude
- not self-seeking
- not easily angered
- forgets the mistakes of others
- not delighting in evil
- rejoices with the truth
- protects
- trusts
- hopes
- perseveres
- never fails

Throughout the New Testament, we read the command to love one another. Following the previous sixteen actions is the best way to do so.

Think about this the next time you profess—or are about to profess—your love for someone else.

Even more important, consider if this list of actions is how you love God.

Who do we love? How can we love them better by applying Paul's definition of the word? Do our actions confirm our love for God?

[Discover more about loving others and loving God in Matthew 22:36–40, Mark 12:28–31, Luke 10:27, and Galatians 5:14.]

DAY 20: THE GREATEST OF THESE IS LOVE
1 CORINTHIANS 13:11–13

And now these three remain: faith, hope and love. But the greatest of these is love. (1 Corinthians 13:13)

In the Old Testament, we have 613 instructions of what to do and not to do (Exodus through Deuteronomy). That's a lot of rules. Among these, God places the focus on ten big ones, the Ten Commandments (Exodus 20:2–17 and Deuteronomy 5:6–21). Centuries later, Jesus narrows it down to just two: love God and love others (Matthew 22:37–39). Paul later confirms that love trumps all else, that it's our greatest pursuit, even more important than faith and hope.

Instead of focusing on what we should and

shouldn't do—following a list of requirements with religious fervor—we should instead turn our attention to the greatest commandment: love.

Love God and love others. If we do this, everything else falls into place.

A song from my youth is "They'll Know We Are Christians," better known as "They'll Know We Are Christians by Our Love." It's based on John 13:35, which says that everyone will know we are Jesus's disciples by how well we love one another. The song's chorus became my anthem, persisting as my guide for life and living.

In Paul's popular teaching on love in 1 Corinthians 13, he ends by saying that three things will last forever: faith, hope, and love. In this trio, love stands above the other two. That means love is the greatest thing.

Yet many in the Western Church esteem knowledge over all else, despite Paul saying love is more important. Paul also elevates love over several other spiritual abilities, such as being able to supernaturally speak in other languages (tongues), give prophetic words, have spiritual discernment, exercise deep faith, possess a giving heart, and endure physical hardship.

Although these pursuits have value, they aren't

as important as simply loving one another. In fact, without love, these other things don't even matter.

I've often seen well-intentioned followers of Jesus seek an impartation of supernatural gifts, especially speaking in tongues, but I've heard no one plead with God for more love. Yet if we apply what Paul says, love should be the first thing we seek.

After all, Paul says that love is the greatest of all.

What secondary quests must we deemphasize so that we can elevate love as our greatest pursuit? How can we better love others?

[Discover more about love in Romans 5:8, 1 Corinthians 8:1, Galatians 5:14, James 2:8, 1 Peter 4:8, and 1 John 4:7–21, as well as in over 600 other verses throughout the Bible.]

DAY 21: BUILD UP THE CHURCH
1 CORINTHIANS 14:1–25

Since you are eager for gifts of the Spirit, try to excel in those that build up the church. (1 Corinthians 14:12)

In his first letter to the church in Corinth, Paul has much to say about the gifts of the Spirit and their proper use. This suggests that the Corinthian church struggles in this area, especially with the misuse of speaking in tongues.

In 1 Corinthians 12, Paul first teaches about spiritual gifts—supernatural abilities that God gives us—for building up Jesus's church and enabling us to function in unity as one body.

In the next chapter, Paul shifts his attention to

something greater than gifts of the Spirit, something far more important. He talks about the more essential attributes of faith, hope, and love, with love standing above the other two. This elevates the importance of love over spiritual gifts, diminishing them in the process. After all, if we don't love others, nothing else matters (1 Corinthians 13:2–3).

In the next section of his letter (1 Corinthians 14), Paul opens with a command for the church in Corinth to pursue love. After that, he wants them to desire the gifts of the Spirit, especially prophecy, which he elevates over speaking in tongues.

In Chapter 17, "Thirteen Spiritual Gifts," we defined prophecy as to "guide others by speaking truth to cause correction or repentance." (Note that the New Testament understanding of prophecy differs from the Old Testament use, which proclaims future events.)

Combining all this, let's look at the hierarchy of spiritual importance. At the top of the list, we have love, the overarching, principal practice that we should all pursue. Of the three enduring characteristics of faith, hope, and love, love is the most important.

After faith, hope, and love, we have the gifts of

Love Is Patient

the Spirit. But not just any spiritual gift. Prophecy is the one Paul deems as most important, much more so than speaking in tongues. Though Paul speaks in tongues and wishes everyone else did so too, he notes its limitations as being something between the speaker and God. It doesn't have any benefit for the other people present—that is, building up the church—unless someone is there to interpret what the speaker says.

Only once have I ever heard someone speak in tongues where the interpretation followed. This, however, is the proper way for this gift to occur in a church gathering. Lacking an interpretation, the person with the gift of tongues should remain quiet, yielding to those with a prophecy to share (1 Corinthians 14:27–28).

That's because prophecy benefits everyone, whereas speaking in tongues doesn't edify anybody. To put this in perspective, Paul says he would rather speak five words that everyone understands than utter 10,000 words that no one comprehends.

We should follow Paul's example and excel in those gifts of the Spirit that build up Jesus's church.

Do we need to re-prioritize love as more important than spiritual gifts? What can we do to best build up Jesus's church?

[Discover more about how God equips us in Ephesians 4:11–13, 2 Timothy 3:16–17, and Hebrews 13:20–21.]

DAY 22: WHEN YOU COME TOGETHER
1 CORINTHIANS 14:26–40

When you come together, each of you has a hymn, or a word of instruction, a revelation, a tongue or an interpretation. Everything must be done so that the church may be built up.
(1 Corinthians 14:26)

Continuing his teaching about church gatherings, Paul lists five activities to do when we come together. But before we look at them, let's consider two key points to inform the subject.

First, Paul says *when* you meet, not *if* you meet. This reminds us that getting together with other followers of Jesus should be a regular occurrence (Hebrews 10:25).

This idea of meeting together can happen anytime. The Bible doesn't specify the day or hour we should meet. Gathering on Sunday morning is merely a practice that developed over time.

Next, Paul says, "each of you." This means everyone, suggesting a gathering where each person contributes and ministers to each other. Everyone taking part removes the division between leaders and attendees, where a few people lead and most people watch. Paul wants everyone involved.

With this as a framework, Paul lists five activities for our church meetings.

1. **Sing a Song**: When we gather, we should sing a hymn or share a song. This could mean playing an instrument so that others can sing along, but more likely it means launching into a song or chorus a cappella as the Holy Spirit leads. This requires no preparation at all, just a willingness to listen for Holy Spirit direction.

2. **Teach a Lesson**: The same approach applies to giving a word of instruction. We don't need to preach a long sermon. Less is more. We can often communicate much by speaking little. All we need is a willingness to share something God taught us during the week or that we learned through

studying Scripture. Everyone can do this. Again, no preparation required.

3. **Share a Revelation**: The idea of having a revelation to share will seem normal to some and strange to others, but a revelation is insight that God has given to us. It might come from Scripture or the Holy Spirit. Paul wants us to share this with those gathered.

The last two items on this list may or may not be common or comfortable activities for you.

4. **Speak in Tongues**: Paul instructs the people in Corinth to speak in tongues. It's biblical, and we should consider this for our church gatherings. But it may be optional, because Paul later says, *if* anyone speaks in tongues. This implies it's not required. But he does say that if people speak in tongues, only a few people should do it and then one at a time.

5. **Interpret the Tongue**: After someone speaks in an unknown language, someone must interpret it. If no one can interpret the message, then the person shouldn't share it. After all, how can words no one understands build up the church?

To conclude his list of five items, Paul says everything we do at our gatherings is to build up the church, to strengthen the faith and community of those present. We should humble ourselves and do things for our common good. This will advance the kingdom of God and the good news of Jesus.

What should we do differently when we come together? How can we reform our church practices to better align with Paul's teachings?

[Discover where else Paul uses the phrase "come together" in 1 Corinthians 11:18, 1 Corinthians 11:20–21, and 1 Corinthians 14:23.]

DAY 23: ALIVE IN JESUS
1 CORINTHIANS 15:1–34

For as in Adam all die, so in Christ all will be made alive.
(1 Corinthians 15:22)

In the story of Adam and Eve eating fruit from the forbidden tree, most people blame Eve for the couple's disobedience, expulsion from the Garden of Eden, and eventual death. Yet I see both as culpable. Both are at fault, even though Adam denounces Eve and Eve condemns the serpent for their wrongdoing.

Through Adam and Eve, sin enters our world and becomes part of humanity through all generations. The punishment for their sin—and ours—is death. This is the reality we live in.

Paul, however, doesn't blame Adam *and* Eve. In this letter to the church in Corinth, he pins the fault solely on Adam. (Interestingly, two other times Paul *does* blame Eve. See 2 Corinthians 11:3 and 1 Timothy 2:14.)

As a consequence of their disobedience, Adam and Eve both die. Because of the sin of the first man and first woman, everyone in succeeding generations throughout time also faces death. This means you, and this means me.

Though this problem of sin and death starts with Adam, it ends with Jesus.

Just as we die because of Adam, we are made alive through Jesus. This is the gospel—the good news—that saves us, and which Paul proclaims.

Because of Adam and Eve's sin, the Old Testament overflows with partial remedies to make up for their disobedience, to atone for their sin. One key solution is through periodic sin offerings, an animal sacrifice (Exodus 29:36, Leviticus 9:7, and many other verses).

Jesus comes and dies as the ultimate sin sacrifice for us to end all sin sacrifices. Yet there's more. To prove his authority to be the final sacrifice, he overcomes death and rises from the dead. Death doesn't keep him in the tomb. His power conquers death.

Love Is Patient

Though each of us still faces death as the end of our life here on earth, through Jesus and his once-and-for-all sacrifice, we too can rise again to live forever. Through Jesus, death isn't the end for us but the transition into a new beginning.

The Corinthian church must struggle in their comprehension of the resurrection, for Paul goes into much detail to explain it from a logical perspective and a theological standpoint. Though Paul addresses resurrection a couple of other times, he mentions it more often and covers it more thoroughly in 1 Corinthians than in all his other letters combined.

Though the Corinthian church struggles to grasp the importance of Jesus's resurrection, thanks to Paul's writing, we don't need to.

Jesus died to save us from our sins and rose again so that we, too, can rise from our death and live with him forever.

How can Jesus's resurrection encourage us in our daily living? How can our hope in life after death influence what we do today?

[Discover more about Adam's sin and Jesus's salvation in Romans 5:12–21. Read other passages about resurrection in Philippians 3:10–11, 2 Timothy 2:18, 1 Peter 1:3, and 1 Peter 3:21.]

DIG DEEPER: CAN WE BE BAPTIZED FOR DEAD PEOPLE?

If the dead are not raised at all, why are people baptized for them? (1 Corinthians 15:29)

A perplexing verse in Paul's letter to his friends in Corinth mentions being baptized for dead people. What in the world does this mean? It sounds heretical.

In grappling with this verse, let's keep two things in mind.

First, we should assume it's a reference to a matter confronting only the church in Corinth, since the Bible doesn't mention it anywhere else. Though we don't know the background of this issue, we do know the Corinthian church has many problems, with this being one of them.

Let's not make this our issue by adopting their misguided practice. After all, they have many unwise habits.

Second, and most importantly, is that Paul shares this action descriptively. He simply says what some people do. Paul does not command them to do this. He does not recommend this. And he does not model this.

Can we be baptized for dead people? I suppose so, but we shouldn't expect it to accomplish anything. This is because baptism is an action someone does publicly to show their commitment to Jesus. A dead person cannot make this decision. It's too late for them.

Should we be baptized for dead people? I think not. Instead of being baptized for someone when they're dead, we will accomplish much more by telling them about Jesus while they're alive.

If we did everything Scripture describes, we'd be a sorry lot. Instead, let's look at what the Bible commands. This will keep us busy for a long time.

Who can we tell about Jesus? What commands in the Bible are we not following as we should?

[Discover more about baptism in Mark 1:8, Mark 16:16, Luke 3:16, Acts 19:4–6, and Romans 6:4.]

DAY 24: DO GOD'S WORK
1 CORINTHIANS 15:35–58

Always give yourselves fully to the work of the Lord, because you know that your labor in the Lord is not in vain.
(1 Corinthians 15:58)

As Paul winds down his first letter to the church in Corinth, he gives a simple command, followed by some encouragement.

He says for them—and by extension, for us—to remain diligent in doing God's work, to give themselves fully to it. Though we may not see the results as we practice this—or at least we might not realize the full outcomes of our actions—we will not toil needlessly. Our labor will produce results. It will not be in vain.

While this command to give God 100 percent of our efforts is simple in concept, *how* to do it presents a challenge.

What does it mean to give ourselves fully to God's work?

Do we need to be employed in full-time ministry at a church or a Christian service organization to do God's work? What if we volunteer our time? Does that count?

Can we do God's work in a regular job, apart from ministry or Christian service? Can we do God's work at school? At home? For our neighbors? With our family?

The answer to each option is yes.

This brings up the next question.

What is God's work?

Is the Lord's work being a pastor or missionary? Is God's work serving at a church? How about helping at a local service organization?

Can we do the work of the Lord as we live our life each day? Of course, we can.

As we go about our daily lives, we can use words to tell others about him. But we may communicate

Love Is Patient

more effectively if we let our actions speak for us. Isn't that God's work too? Yes, indeed.

Though some people waste time debating what it means to do the Lord's work and in what setting we should do it, don't let them impede the command to give ourselves fully to what we do for God. When we do this, we know our efforts won't be in vain.

May this guide us in all that we do and all that we say.

How can we fully do the work of the Lord? How can we best use our present situation to make sure our labor is not in vain?

[Discover more about working for our Lord in Romans 16:12, 1 Corinthians 16:10, Colossians 3:23, and 1 Thessalonians 5:12.]

DAY 25: IF IT'S GOD'S WILL
1 CORINTHIANS 16:1–24

I hope to spend some time with you, if the Lord permits.
(1 Corinthians 16:7)

In the concluding section of Paul's letter, he mentions many people. These include Timothy, Apollos, Stephanas, Fortunatus, Achaicus, Aquila, and Priscilla. We could dive into the lives of each one of them to receive encouragement in how we live and grow in our faith. (I look at each one of these people in my book *The Friends and Foes of Jesus*.)

Besides Paul mentioning these people, he also outlines his intentions. In one instance, he adds the qualifier "if the Lord permits." Even though I know better, this is a perspective I often forget to embrace and one that I should apply as I schedule each day and envision each year.

This doesn't mean that we shouldn't plan or that we should do nothing, passing off our inaction as waiting for God. That would be lazy.

Only a foolish person would sit at home and say, "If the Lord permits, I'll buy food today." Instead, the wise person—the person who doesn't want to go hungry—plans to buy food and then acts accordingly. An even wiser person buys food but does so understanding that they will accomplish their goal only if God allows it.

After all, the Almighty may have other plans for our day, which will divert us from buying groceries so that we may better accomplish his will. Too often I miss these godly diversions because I'm so focused on pursuing my own goals.

Unlike myself, Paul models this God-honoring perspective well, balancing his plans with the Lord's will. We read about this in the book of Acts. In Paul's travels he has the option to go to Asia, but the Holy Spirit keeps him from doing so. Later he tries to enter Bithynia, but the Spirit of Jesus prohibits him and his group from going there too.

That night Paul has a vision of a man in

Love Is Patient

Macedonia pleading for him to come and help them. Paul sees his dream as God's direction and goes to Macedonia to tell them about Jesus (Acts 16:6–10).

In this we see that Paul plans, but he holds his plans loosely. He listens for Holy Spirit direction and acts accordingly. Paul's intentions serve as a starting point for his day and his travels, providing a general intent for his ministry, but his itinerary is flexible. Instead, he waits for God to fine-tune his goals and even overrule them as needed.

His plans carry the caveat of "if the Lord permits." We should follow Paul's example.

How can we better balance our will with God's? What must we do to better tune in to the direction of the Holy Spirit?

[Discover more about the proper perspective for our plans in James 4:13–16.]

DIG DEEPER: A HOLY KISS

Greet one another with a holy kiss. (1 Corinthians 16:20)

Many churches have a time of greeting in their services. This can range from awkward to engaging.

At most of these churches, people merely shake hands and mumble a rote welcome. Folks in other congregations make eye contact and smile as they greet one another. And at a few places, a meaningful connection occurs.

One church my wife and I visited for my book *52 Churches* carried this to an extreme. The minister told us to "greet one another with a holy kiss." Despite these kisses from strangers being on our cheeks, it was creepy, marking one of our more uncomfortable moments that year. Fortunately, few people attended that Sunday, so the number of holy kisses we received was minimal.

I know this is biblical, with Paul mentioning it four times and Peter, once. But I don't really know what it means. Even after experiencing it, I can't describe it, except to say that it disturbed me. And Paul doesn't explain it or offer instructions. He just says to do it.

It could be that Paul's audience back then understood what he meant. Yet if a kiss of greeting was a societal norm, why did Paul need to instruct the churches to do it? It seems we're missing some details or misunderstanding the context.

We can, however, infer a few things.

First, each time Paul mentions the phrase *holy kiss*, it's in a letter to a church, so it must be just for the church community. I take this to suggest that holy kissing doesn't apply to outsiders or, in our case, visitors.

Next, a kiss is an intimate sign of affection. Since the context is church, we might understand this kiss as spiritual affection rather than an act of physical intimacy.

Last, as a holy act, it's something sacred. It is not sexual or disingenuous.

Combining these implies a holy kiss is a sacred act of spiritual intimacy for people in a church community, but I still don't know how to do it.

Could it be that the details are up to us to decide?

How can we effectively greet other believers with a holy kiss? How can we do this without it being unsettling or inappropriate? Should we even try?

[Discover three other times Paul writes about greeting one another with a holy kiss in Romans 16:16, 2 Corinthians 13:12, and 1 Thessalonians 5:26. Read Peter's command to do so in 1 Peter 5:14.]

DAY 26: WHEN PEOPLE PRAY
2 CORINTHIANS 1:1–2:4

He has delivered us from such a deadly peril, and he will deliver us again. (2 Corinthians 1:10)

Paul opens his second letter to the church in Corinth (or at least the second letter we have record of) with a personal update—from a spiritual perspective—on what has happened since he last wrote to them. He praises God for deliverance from difficulty.

The hardship that he and his ministry companions endured was most significant. He says it weighed on their hearts as a death sentence. Imagine trying to tell others the good news about

Jesus with a deep dread hanging over you like a cloud, able to unleash a deadly torrent in an instant.

But despite the great distress this threat brought on them, Paul nevertheless sees a positive result. It teaches him and his team to not rely on themselves and their own abilities to accomplish God's purpose. Instead, they are to rely on God, mindful that he raises people from the dead. As a result, the impending threat of death means nothing when they place their trust in resurrected Jesus, who can resurrect others. God may have already done this once for Paul (see Acts 14:19–20).

Given this, Paul gives a confident declaration of what has occurred and affirms his belief in what will happen. What is his testimony? That God has delivered him and his companions from the threat of death once, and he will do it again.

Paul isn't assuming that God will keep them from receiving death threats, but he knows that when these warnings occur, God will deliver them from the assault. This is a testament to Paul's faith and his trust in God to protect them as they tell others about Jesus.

There's one more item, however, tacked on to this truth that's easy to miss. Paul says God will

Love Is Patient

continue to deliver them from threats as the Corinthian church continues to pray (2 Corinthians 1:11).

This is significant. The people of the church in Corinth, for all their many struggles, have prayed and are praying for Paul and his missionary team. He acknowledges that their prayers help him to push forward.

This should encourage us to pray for our church leaders and missionaries when they request it—and even when they don't. Paul affirms the value he places on the prayers of others and God's answers to their petitions.

May we remember this the next time someone asks us to pray for them. Don't say yes and forget. Don't pray once and then stop. Pray and continue to pray. In this way, we will help others through our prayers, just as the Corinthians helped Paul.

Thank you, Jesus, for hearing our prayers and for the answers you provide.

How can we be more diligent about praying for people when they request it? How can we be more intentional about praying for people even when they don't ask for it?

[Discover more about Paul facing death in Acts 27:22–25 and 2 Corinthians 11:24–27.]

DAY 27: RESTORATION
2 CORINTHIANS 2:5–3:6

Now instead, you ought to forgive and comfort him, so that he will not be overwhelmed by excessive sorrow.
(2 Corinthians 2:7)

In Chapter 6, "Judge Others or Not," we talked about a man in the Corinthian church actively engaging in incest and proud of it. The other followers of Jesus condone his actions. Paul tells the church in Corinth to have nothing to do with this man, to mourn his actions and put him out of their fellowship. We would be overreaching if we conclude that we should shun everyone in our church whom we judge as having sinned—after all, none of us is without fault. Paul, however, takes issue with sexually immoral people within Jesus's church.

Though Paul doesn't make an implicit connection, we can logically link the passage on forgiveness in 2 Corinthians with his instruction to ostracize the sexually immoral man in 1 Corinthians.

Unlike most of us today with many options of where to go to church, this man has just one: Jesus's only church in Corinth. By removing him from their fellowship, the church eliminates his ability to take part in spiritual community.

Paul now determines the man has suffered enough. We don't know how Paul reaches this conclusion, whether the Holy Spirit directs him in this decision or if he receives a report of the man's contrition. But what we do know is that the man's ouster isn't permanent, only temporary.

Now it's time to welcome him back. Paul tells the church to forgive the man for his sins, even though they're deplorable. Paul wants them to comfort this sexually immoral person so that sorrow doesn't overwhelm him. Paul wants the church to reaffirm their love for this man.

Welcoming him back into their fellowship reinstates him into a faith community. This is key, for without a connection with other believers, he could

Love Is Patient

easily wander from his faith or even turn his back on Jesus.

I've heard of this happening too often in today's church. A person engages in what the church deems a sexual sin or struggles with a temptation to do so. Instead of incest, however, as in the church of Corinth, the issue today is often homosexuality.

The church, either formally or effectively, pushes this person out of their congregation. Without a spiritual connection and a faith community to provide encouragement, they are forced to suffer alone and often walk away from God.

If only each one of these churches had welcomed this person back, offering comfort and reaffirming their love. Had they done so—as Paul instructed the Corinthians—they could have restored this person to their faith instead of driving them away from it and into the embrace of a world who accepts them and loves them as they are.

This is a thorny issue to navigate, but with Paul's instructions to the church in Corinth as an example and the Holy Spirit to guide us we can appropriately discern the right path to take.

How should we best react to someone who deviates from our conventions? What can we do to help them stay on their faith journey and not veer off course?

[Discover more about restoration in Galatians 6:1 and 1 Peter 5:10–11.]

DIG DEEPER: PEDDLE GOD FOR PROFIT

We do not peddle the word of God for profit.
(2 Corinthians 2:17)

An oft-repeated criticism against today's Western church is that "they're only after your money." Regardless of the accuracy of this statement, donations fuel the church and money motivates ministers and missionaries alike. It's only a question of how much. Few are immune to this in our materialistic, money-driven world.

Though Paul establishes that missionaries are worthy of compensation, he also boasts that he pays his own way, working for a living so he can provide Jesus for free. Although lofty, this example is a worthy pursuit for anyone in ministry. Yet, we must balance this with the principle of receiving appropriate pay.

Though a few go into ministry with selfish, profit motives from the start, others slide into this mindset over time, establishing excessive lifestyles for which they have no need, seeking only to satiate an unfulfilled craving for more. They end up peddling God's Word to produce a profit.

We shouldn't conclude from this, however, that Jesus's leaders should live a life of poverty—unless that's what God calls them to do, and they do so willingly. However, we need to guard against supporting spiritual leaders who live a lavish lifestyle, or one far removed from the living conditions of their donors.

We must watch out for preachers who peddle God for profit. When we encounter such a person, we should redirect our attention—and our funds—to a more worthy cause.

How can we best discern what ministry or parachurch

organization to follow and support? What must we do to be good stewards of the money God has provided us with?

[Discover more about people peddling God for profit in John 2:14–16. Read about the love of money in 1 Timothy 6:10.]

DAY 28: FREEDOM
2 CORINTHIANS 3:7–18

Where the Spirit of the Lord is, there is freedom.
(2 Corinthians 3:17)

There's a story in the Old Testament about Moses. After fasting for forty days and nights and spending time with God on Mount Sinai, he returns with the Ten Commandments and other instructions. His countenance glows because of being in God's presence. When the people see his radiance, they pull back in fear. He later puts a veil over his face. This is so the people won't have to look at his shining aura. Whenever he spends time with God, he removes the veil and then puts it back on when he's around people (Exodus 34:29–35). The veil keeps the people from seeing God through Moses.

There's another veil in the Bible that keeps the people from seeing God. This veil is in the temple. It separates the temple's holiest area—where God is present—from the people in the rest of the temple and the courtyard surrounding it.

When Jesus dies, this curtain in the temple tears in two. The Bible notes that it rips from top to bottom. This symbolically shows God initiating the removal of this man-made separation between him and his people (Mark 15:37–39). It's as if God opens the door of his home to grant us access.

This is the historical context behind this verse about the freedom we have through the Spirit of the Lord. We have freedom because of Jesus and through the Holy Spirit. No longer are we separated from God and bound to the law. Because of Jesus, we're released from striving to obey a lengthy list of rules that give us actions to do and activities to avoid. We are free from the Old Testament's legalistic approach to God.

Since Jesus set us free, we must resist the attempts of others to pile various requirements on us, making us slaves to their rules. This load (yoke) is a heavy burden that enslaves us to their narrow-

Love Is Patient

minded perspectives (Galatians 5:1). Remember, we have freedom through the Holy Spirit.

Does this freedom give us the liberty to do whatever we want? It may, but don't go there. That's the wrong perspective. More correctly, we have the freedom to do good. We don't pursue right behavior to earn God's approval. Instead, it's a response to what he did for us. This isn't an act of obligation but the result of a thankful heart.

We can do good because we want to. We shouldn't view our Holy Spirit freedom as a cover for evil (1 Peter 2:15–17). We're free to do right.

How should we understand our freedom through the Holy Spirit? How can we best use our freedom to do good?

[Discover more about freedom in Luke 4:18, Romans 8:20–21, and Galatians 2:4.]

DAY 29: EASY OR HARD?
2 CORINTHIANS 4:1–18

We are hard pressed on every side, but not crushed; perplexed, but not in despair; persecuted, but not abandoned; struck down, but not destroyed. (2 Corinthians 4:8–9)

Paul warns the church in Corinth not to deceive others or distort God's word (2 Corinthians 4:2). That is, don't misrepresent God's character or intent to the world.

Yet this happens. A lot. Some people, in their zeal for Jesus, promise those on the outside looking in that if they just say yes to Jesus all their problems will go away, and life will become easy.

But this isn't what the Bible says. Salvation

doesn't remove our problems. In fact, we should realize that aligning ourselves with Jesus will make our life more difficult, not easier.

Jesus knows this. He tells those who are interested in following him to count the cost before committing their life to him (Luke 14:28–33). This is because his followers will pay a price for their commitment to him.

Paul details this heavy cost, but along with each threat he gives assurance of God's provision.

- First, we will find ourselves hard pressed from every direction but not crushed. God will make sure we can stand up under the pressures we face from the world and from the enemy.
- Next, we will find ourselves perplexed but not in despair. Though we won't understand everything about our faith journey or life circumstances, we do not need to react in dismay, because God is with us.
- Third, we'll find ourselves persecuted but not abandoned. Yes, people will mistreat us and attack us because they

don't like Jesus or can't accept his message. But God will not forget us when these assaults occur. He'll remember us in our dark times and won't leave us on our own.

- Last, we will find ourselves struck down but not destroyed. Though we may struggle under the assaults of others as we follow Jesus, this will not ruin us. Through God, we stand strong.

This means that when we follow Jesus and live for him, we can expect to be harassed, confused, attacked, and hurt. Yet in this, God promises we will not be defeated, anguished, forgotten, or ruined.

Yes, we must count the cost before we promise to follow Jesus, because committing ourselves to him may bring about hardship. But we can take courage knowing that God will prevail and help us through these trying situations.

Regardless of our circumstances, God walks with us and will never leave us.

Do we think following Jesus should be easy or hard? When

we face hardships, do we run from them or trust God to deliver us?

[Discover more about the cost of following Jesus in Matthew 10:37–38, Luke 9:23, Luke 10:3, Galatians 2:20, and Colossians 3:2–3.]

DAY 30: LIVE BY FAITH
2 CORINTHIANS 5:1–10

For we live by faith, not by sight. (2 Corinthians 5:7)

One outcome of the modern age was separating the secular from the spiritual. As people elevated the physical—what they could see and count—over what they couldn't witness or quantify, an empirical mindset emerged. If something wasn't tangible, they would dismiss it or even ignore it. This resulted in people living their life by sight—that is, through logic.

The opposite approach is living life by faith, which modern thought relegated to Sunday mornings and effectively pushed out of society, where it remains for much of our world.

This idea of living by sight and not by faith, however, transcends the modern era. Two thousand years ago, the disciple Thomas also exemplified this perspective. Absent when Jesus first reveals himself to the other disciples, Thomas refuses to believe their testimony that Jesus rose from the grave, that their once-dead Savior is dead no more and alive again. From a logical perspective, Jesus's resurrection makes no sense to the rational-thinking disciple. He demands proof. And Jesus will soon provide it.

A week later, the disciples—along with Thomas—gather again. Behind locked doors, Jesus suddenly appears in their midst. After blessing them with peace, he talks directly to the doubting disciple. "Touch the nail holes in my hand and the opening in my side." Then he tells Thomas—along with everyone throughout history who hesitates to accept his message—to "Stop doubting and start believing."

Thomas does what Jesus says. He sees and then believes, embracing Jesus as his Lord and God (John 20:24–29).

Jesus affirms him for seeing and believing. Even more so, Jesus affirms those who haven't seen the evidence of his resurrection but believe anyway. I'm

Love Is Patient

one of those people who believes in Jesus without seeing tangible evidence. I hope you are too.

Believing in Jesus is our first act of faith. But belief isn't a once-and-done action. We confirm our initial decision to believe by following Jesus every day. Some may attempt to do so with a modern-era perspective, walking with Jesus by sight, but this so limits them on their journey with him.

Instead, Paul calls the church in Corinth to a higher standard, one that we can all embrace. He tells them that instead of living by what they tangibly see, they should instead live by faith—the things they cannot see.

When we put our trust in Jesus, we take our first step of faith. When we travel through life with him at our side each day, we best accomplish by walking in faith.

What can we do to better live by faith and not by sight? How can we encourage others to live by faith?

[Discover more about faith in Romans 4:5, 2 Thessalonians 1:3, Hebrews 11:1, and James 5:15.]

DAY 31: GOD'S NEW CREATION
2 CORINTHIANS 5:11–6:2

Therefore, if anyone is in Christ, the new creation has come: The old has gone, the new is here! (2 Corinthians 5:17)

The biblical account starts with our creation in Genesis 1 and 2. After each stage of his handiwork, God proclaims the results as "good." On day six, when he fashions people—male and female, created in his image—he surveys all that he has made, and this time pronounces it as "very good" (Genesis 1:31).

Yet it may not be good enough. Here's why. In Jesus and through Jesus we can become a *new* creation, implicitly better than God's original version. If the Genesis creation was very good, what does that make us as his new creation through Jesus? How about exceptionally good?

To become God's new creation, we must believe in and follow Jesus. This transitions us from God's original creation into his new creation. But there's more. As God's new creation in Christ, the old way disappears, and a new perspective emerges. This marks our spiritual transformation.

Paul understands this well. He made a significant transformation from his old approach of harassing, hunting, and killing Jesus's followers. Replacing this he becomes a zealous follower of Christ, who endures much to encounter, convert, and instruct people about salvation through Jesus.

Like Paul, as a new creation in Jesus, our old approach to living goes away. We no longer find ourselves enslaved to sin. Though evil and the temptation to do wrong still surround us, we now comprehend them from a new perspective, one we receive in Christ and through Christ. Day by day we persevere in becoming this new creation through Jesus. We move toward perfection.

The Old Testament recognizes humanity's sins and prescribes a lengthy set of rules of what to do and not do. Yet no one can completely follow these commands. If we stumble just once, we're as guilty as if we fail every time (James 2:10).

The Old Testament ordered recurring animal sacrifices as sin offerings to address the people's shortcomings. In the New Testament, Jesus comes to fulfill the Old Testament's way. He becomes the ultimate sacrifice, the once-and-for-all payment for all sins throughout all time. Through him we can become a new creation; the old system disappears, replaced by Jesus's fresh approach.

This makes us God's new creation.

How does being a new creation in Christ affect how we live? Do our actions and attitudes prove we really believe the old is gone, and the new has come?

[Discover more about creation in Romans 1:20, Romans 8:22, Galatians 6:15, and Ephesians 1:4.]

DAY 32: PAUL'S COMMENDATION
2 CORINTHIANS 6:3–13

Rather, as servants of God we commend ourselves in every way . . . (2 Corinthians 6:4)

When I encounter the word *commend* in Paul's letter, it's a speed bump. Not only does it slow down my reading of the passage, but it confuses me. I envision Paul pointing a proud thumb at his puffed-up chest, bragging about all he has done. Indeed, this is the primary definition of the word commend: to express approval or praise. It seems Paul is praising himself. But this is not the case.

A secondary definition of commend is to represent as qualified or worthy of recommendation. To confirm this understanding, some other translations of this verse use the words show, exhibit, approve, and demonstrate.

Given this understanding of Paul's use of the word *commend*, the six verses that follow it emerge as validating his work.

He starts by listing eight facts that confirm his integrity and that of his team's ministry:

1. They must persevere in telling others the good news of Jesus ("in great endurance," verse 4).
2. Their journey is difficult ("in troubles, hardships and distresses," verse 4).
3. They suffer physically ("in beatings, imprisonments and riots," verse 5).
4. They go without ("in hard work, sleepless nights and hunger," verse 5).
5. Nevertheless, they persist in right living ("in purity, understanding, patience and kindness," verse 6).
6. They're guided by the Holy Spirit and love ("in the Holy Spirit and in sincere love," verse 6).

Love Is Patient

7. They speak truth through God's power ("in truthful speech and in the power of God," verse 7).
8. They fight evil that pushes in from all directions with good ("with weapons of righteousness in the right hand and in the left," verse 7).

Following this list, Paul adds nine paradoxes, which contrast conflicting reactions to his ministry:

1. Honored but attacked ("through glory and dishonor," verse 8).
2. Slandered but affirmed ("bad report and good report," verse 8).
3. Authentic but disregarded ("genuine, yet treated as impostors," verse 8).
4. Recognized but dismissed ("known, yet regarded as unknown," verse 9).
5. Facing death but living ("dying, and yet we live on," verse 9).
6. Broken but not dead ("beaten, and yet not killed," verse 9).
7. Celebrating despite distress ("sorrowful, yet always rejoicing," verse 10).

8. Making sacrifices for others ("poor, yet making many rich," verse 10).
9. Being destitute in this world but rich in the next ("having nothing, and yet possessing everything," verse 10).

These stand as Paul's testimony, validating his ministry to the Corinthian church and setting an example for us to follow. The fact that Paul feels the need to list his credentials and remind the people in Corinth of his qualifications and dedication suggest that they question his authority as their spiritual leader.

It's appropriate for us to ensure the people we follow on our spiritual journey and who lead us at our churches are worthy of our attention. Yet we need to make sure we're not overly critical and force them to commend themselves to us after years of faithful service. The church in Corinth seems to have erred in this regard. May we not repeat their mistake.

Can we commend ourselves the way Paul does? What must we change to better tell others about Jesus?

[Discover another time Paul commends himself in 2 Corinthians 11:16–33.]

DAY 33: YOKED WITH UNBELIEVERS
2 CORINTHIANS 6:14–7:1

Do not be yoked together with unbelievers. For what do righteousness and wickedness have in common? Or what fellowship can light have with darkness? (2 Corinthians 6:14)

Paul warns the church in Corinth to not yoke themselves—that is, to align themselves—with people who don't believe in Jesus. The image of a yoke applies to two animals paired together, working as a team to pull a heavy load.

To do so effectively, they must be of equal strength. They certainly need to move in the same direction and at the same time if their efforts are to be effective. This is how a yoke works to produce optimum results.

But moving beyond the image of animals, what does it mean to yoke a believer with an unbeliever? We can obviously conclude that doing so won't be ideal or provide effective results, but let's look for some examples.

Preachers often apply this verse to marriage, for a person who follows Jesus to not marry someone who doesn't believe. This makes sense. But while this may be a sound application, it isn't absolute. In the next chapter, Paul notes that a believing spouse may save their unbelieving partner (1 Corinthians 7:16), something Peter echoes (1 Peter 3:1). This doesn't, however, give permission to marry an unbeliever, but for situations where one person in a marriage decides to follow Jesus and the other person doesn't—at least not right away.

I've also seen this verse wrongly used by asserting, for example, that a Baptist can't marry a Lutheran, a Protestant can't marry a Catholic, or a person of one race can't marry someone of another race. Assuming each person follows Jesus, this grossly misapplies Paul's instruction.

Another application relates to business, for a Christian businessperson to avoid forming partnerships with non-Christians. Again, there is wisdom in this, but it isn't absolute either.

Instead, let's look at Paul's contrasts that come from a mismatched yoke (2 Corinthians 6:14–16):

- Right living versus wrong living
- Light versus darkness
- Jesus versus those opposed to him
- A believer versus an unbeliever
- God versus idols

Instead of applying this passage to marriage or business, let's focus on the final contrast of God versus idols, something the preceding phrases build up to. What if the primary intent of Paul's writing is a warning to not yoke the God of the Bible with other religions?

Mixing diverse spiritual practices is a popular trend these days. People take what they like about Christianity, stir in some Eastern religions, add a bit of Judaism or Islam, and season it with some ideas of their own. An example might be making up your own religion using transcendental meditation, crystals, and tarot cards, along with the teachings of Jesus.

The result is a manmade religion, an idol of your own making. God is not pleased.

The Bible warns us not to place God and idols under the same yoke. Don't mix God with anything else.

How can we best apply the idea of an unequal yoke to our lives? Have we yoked wrong spiritual activities to Jesus?

[Discover more about idol worship in 2 Kings 17:12, Psalm 97:7, Psalm 106:36, Isaiah 44:15–17, and Revelation 9:20.]

DAY 34: GODLY SORROW
2 CORINTHIANS 7:2–16

Godly sorrow brings repentance that leads to salvation and leaves no regret, but worldly sorrow brings death.
(2 Corinthians 7:10)

Sorrow is an emotion I seek to avoid. Maybe you do too. I don't want to endure the mental suffering caused by loss, disappointment, or misfortune. I prefer to focus on things that bring me joy. But Paul instructs the church in Corinth about sorrow, so I'll listen to what he says.

The theme of sorrow occurs throughout the Bible, but Paul mentions it more times in this chapter than in any other chapter in the Bible.

Given this, we'll do well to consider what he teaches on the subject.

He talks about the Corinthians' deep sorrow over an unspecified issue, but which may relate to the incestuous situation we discussed in Chapter 6, "Judge Others or Not." Regardless, Paul notes that his earlier letter, which we assume is 1 Corinthians, may have caused this sorrow, but he doesn't regret it. Their sorrow had a purpose, accomplishing Paul's aim of producing repentance. Though this passage may seem cryptic to us, I'm sure Paul's message was clear and meaningful to his audience.

Then Paul throws out the phrase "godly sorrow."

I seldom consider sorrow as godly. Instead, I perceive sorrow as a torment that threatens to pull me away from my Lord and distract me from him.

Yet godly sorrow—our mental anguish over the sinful things we have done—can produce a profound outcome. This is because godly sorrow comes when we realize the mistakes we have made and see how our wrong living separates us from being in a right relationship with God.

When this godly sorrow infiltrates our hearts, we repent. Repentance is a God-honoring response to sorrow. We feel bad for what we have done and decide to pursue a different path. We repent and make a U-turn with our life. Instead of pursuing an inappropriate lifestyle, we do an about-face to pursue Jesus. This leads to our salvation and leaves no room for regret.

The opposite of godly sorrow, however, is worldly sorrow. It accomplishes nothing good. Paul says that worldly sorrow brings about death. A worldly sorrow is any mental suffering that pulls us away from God or threatens our relationship with him.

We all encounter various sorrows in our lives. When we have sorrow over our mistakes, this can either drive us into the saving embrace of Jesus or weigh us down with deadly guilt.

How we respond is up to us.

How should we best react when we feel godly sorrow for our actions? What should we do to avoid worldly sorrow?

[Discover more about sorrow in Matthew 26:36–38, Luke 22:45, Romans 9:1–2, and Philippians 2:25–28.]

DAY 35: GENEROSITY
2 CORINTHIANS 8:1–9:5

But since you excel in everything—in faith, in speech, in knowledge, in complete earnestness and in the love we have kindled in you—see that you also excel in this grace of giving.
(2 Corinthians 8:7)

Much of Paul's instructions to the church in Corinth address their shortcomings, the things they've done wrong. Therefore, when we get to this chapter, it's surprising to read Paul's complimentary words, especially when he says, "since you excel in everything."

At first, we might assume he's using sarcasm to make his point, but a careful reading of this verse reveals his sincerity. He specifies several traits that they excel in. Hearing his affirmation of them encourages me. If a group of people who struggle so much on their spiritual journey can produce these outcomes, we too can hope to experience the same results.

Consider the things Paul praises them for:

- **Faith**: they believe in Jesus and put their eternal trust in him, growing daily (see 2 Corinthians 10:15).
- **Speech**: their words build up and don't tear down, serving as their testimony (see 1 Corinthians 1:5–6).
- **Knowledge**: some of them have Holy Spirit insight (see 1 Corinthians 12:7–10).
- **Earnestness** (sincerity): they are serious about following Jesus and sincere in their devotion to God (see 2 Corinthians 11:3).
- **Love**: they follow Paul's earlier instructions about how to love others (see 1 Corinthians 13:4–7).

These five traits—faith, speech, knowledge,

Love Is Patient

earnestness, and love—provide a noteworthy affirmation of the Corinthian church and stand as admirable characteristics for us to aspire to.

Yet Paul has one more thing to add to this list: the grace of giving, the gracious desire to help others financially. This emerges from the grace—unmerited favor—they've received through Jesus. As a result, Paul encourages them in their collection for the needs of the church in Jerusalem (1 Corinthians 16:1–3).

But Paul isn't trying to manipulate them into giving. He simply urges them to persevere in what they've already pledged to do. He doesn't want them to fall short of the promise they have willingly made.

The Corinthian church, in a better financial situation than the Jerusalem church, could do nothing and remain well off, leaving their brothers and sisters to suffer. Alternately, the Corinthian church could give all they have to the Jerusalem church and suffer for their generosity, while their brothers and sisters live in plenty.

Paul urges an appropriate level of giving, sharing some of their plenty to provide for some of Jerusalem's need. His goal is balance, reminding them of the Israelites gathering manna in the desert. Regardless of how much they harvested, they had exactly what they needed (Exodus 16:18). Earlier, the church in Jerusalem modeled this sharing of possessions with one another (Acts 2:44–45 and Acts 4:32–35).

Paul is not begging for their money or commanding them to give. Instead, he wants them to excel in the grace of giving, just as they said they would.

Are we generous with the things God blesses us with? How can we excel at the grace of giving, just like the Corinthian church?

[Discover more about giving to others in Matthew 6:3–4 and Romans 12:6–8.]

DIG DEEPER: THE OLD TESTAMENT IN 1 AND 2 CORINTHIANS

As it is written . . . (2 Corinthians 8:15)

Paul's two letters to the church in Corinth include many Old Testament references. He knows the Scriptures well. Given his background, this isn't surprising.

First Corinthians has seventeen verses that connect with twenty-two places in the Old Testament. Second Corinthians has ten verses that find support in fourteen Old Testament sections.

Here are the twenty-seven verses in 1 and 2 Corinthians that connect to the Old Testament. Some passages have multiple Old Testament sources.

- 1 Corinthians 1:19 refers to Isaiah 29:14.
- 1 Corinthians 1:31 cites Jeremiah 9:23–24.
- 1 Corinthians 2:9 cites Isaiah 64:4.
- 1 Corinthians 2:16 refers to Isaiah 40:13.
- 1 Corinthians 3:19 quotes Job 5:13.
- 1 Corinthians 3:20 refers to Psalm 94:11.
- 1 Corinthians 5:13 finds support in Deuteronomy 13:5; 17:7; 19:19; 21:21; 22:21, 24; and 24:7.
- 1 Corinthians 6:16 refers to Genesis 2:24.
- 1 Corinthians 9:9 quotes Deuteronomy 25:4.
- 1 Corinthians 10:7 quotes Exodus 32:6.
- 1 Corinthians 10:26 quotes Psalm 24:1.
- 1 Corinthians 14:21 refers to Isaiah 28:11–12.
- 1 Corinthians 15:27 refers to Psalm 8:6.
- 1 Corinthians 15:32 quotes Isaiah 22:13.
- 1 Corinthians 15:45 refers to Genesis 2:7.

Love Is Patient

- 1 Corinthians 15:54 refers to Isaiah 25:8.
- 1 Corinthians 15:55 refers to Hosea 13:14.
- 2 Corinthians 3:7–8 and 13 refer to Exodus 34:29–35.
- 2 Corinthians 4:6 alludes to Genesis 1:3.
- 2 Corinthians 6:2 refers to Isaiah 49:8.
- 2 Corinthians 6:16 finds support in Leviticus 26:12; Jeremiah 32:38; and Ezekiel 37:27.
- 2 Corinthians 6:17 quotes from Isaiah 52:11 and alludes to Ezekiel 20:34, 41.
- 2 Corinthians 6:18 refers to 2 Samuel 7:14.
- 2 Corinthians 8:15 cites Exodus 16:18.
- 2 Corinthians 9:9 quotes Psalm 112:9.
- 2 Corinthians 10:17, which repeats 1 Corinthians 1:31, refers to Jeremiah 9:24.
- 2 Corinthians 13:1 alludes to Deuteronomy 19:15.

It's unlikely Paul could look up these passages when he wrote these two letters. This means he knew the Old Testament well and suggests he memorized it.

How much of the Bible have we memorized? Do we value what the Old Testament says?

[Discover more about studying Scripture in 2 Timothy 3:16–17.]

DAY 36: A CHEERFUL GIVER
2 CORINTHIANS 9:6–15

Each of you should give what you have decided in your heart to give, not reluctantly or under compulsion, for God loves a cheerful giver. (2 Corinthians 9:7)

Paul continues writing about generosity to Jesus's followers in Corinth. He reminds them that if they're stingy when they sow, they will harvest little. Yet if they plant much, they'll reap much (2 Corinthians 9:6). Though the image is of a farmer planting fields in the spring in anticipation of fall's bounty, the allusion is to generous giving to others.

Generosity produces blessing, whereas stinginess results in scarcity. In another letter, this one to the church in Galatia, Paul is more concise: we reap what we sow (Galatians 6:7).

Likewise, Jesus says that if we give freely, we'll receive more. If we cling to what we have, we'll receive less (Matthew 25:29).

So, when we give, we should avoid giving to get. Giving to others to earn a return on our investment is not generosity, but self-centered motivation. When we give so that we may get, we miss the point. God discerns our motives (Proverbs 16:2).

Yes, I know people who gave from their poverty and God repaid them, sometimes one hundredfold. But their blessing seldom came quickly and often involved hardship along the way.

So be generous, but don't give to get something in return. Just give to bless others, and leave the reward up to God.

In the Old Testament, God promised Father Abraham that he and his offspring would be blessed to be a blessing. Everyone on earth would receive a blessing through Abraham (Genesis 12:1–3). Through the patriarch and his descendants, God promises to bless all nations through the ages (Genesis 22:17–18).

Though I am not a physical descendant of Abraham, I consider myself a spiritual descendant,

Love Is Patient

through Jesus. As such, God blesses me so that I may bless others. This goes beyond placing my hand on someone's head and proclaiming, "I bless you in God's name."

Though I pray I will bless others through the words God gives me as I write, I can also bless others through the money he provides.

In the Old Testament, God says he will bless us so we can bless others. In the New Testament, he says when we bless others, he will bless us even more. But as we give generously, may we do so for the right reasons and with a cheerful heart.

God gives his blessings to us because he loves us, and God gives generously to us so we can give generously to others.

Are we doing all we can to be a blessing to others? When we give, do we do so with a cheerful heart?

[Discover more about giving in Proverbs 11:25, Matthew 10:42, Luke 21:1–4, and Luke 6:38.]

DAY 37: TAKE EVERY THOUGHT CAPTIVE
2 CORINTHIANS 10:1–18

We demolish arguments and every pretension that sets itself up against the knowledge of God, and we take captive every thought to make it obedient to Christ. (2 Corinthians 10:5)

Paul tells the church in Corinth to capture every thought and make it subject to Jesus. He encourages them to fight against any notions that are contrary to God. They do this by taking every thought captive and forcing it to submit to Jesus.

Likewise, Proverbs advises us to guard our heart and everything that flows through it (Proverbs 4:23). This includes our thoughts.

As we follow Paul's instructions and contemplate God-honoring ideas, we focus our attention on what is worthwhile. To do this, we start by holding every thought captive to render it obedient to Jesus.

Though hard to do, it is possible.

Although I'm still working on it, my solution is to distract myself from wayward thoughts. When I remember to do this, they usually dissipate quickly. My efforts to divert my attention from wrong thinking take two forms: quoting Scripture and praying.

The first verse that comes to mind is in James: "Resist the devil and he will flee from you" (James 4:7). This is sound advice to follow, but when I remember it, I end up focusing on what I'm trying to escape from. It doesn't help me control my every thought.

Instead, my go-to verse is from Revelation: "Holy, holy, holy is the Lord God Almighty, who was, and is, and is to come" (Revelation 4:8). This passage places my focus on God, praising him, worshiping him, and acknowledging his eternal existence. The enemy doesn't like this. And he flees.

I end up reciting this verse almost every day, often multiple times.

Another way to distract ourselves from wrong thinking is to pray. The enemy doesn't like that

Love Is Patient

either. However, it doesn't work for me to pray that I'll stop thinking wrong thoughts or for strength to hold them captive. This also focuses my attention on what I'm trying to avoid. Instead, we can pray for someone else.

Just as I have one predetermined verse, I have one predetermined person I automatically pray for when wrong thoughts beckon. This keeps me from wasting time trying to decide who to pray for and gets me to the praying part quickly. After praying for this person, God often directs me to intercede for others.

Capturing every thought and subjecting it to Jesus is possible when we recite Scripture and pray. The key is to remember to do so.

What else can we do to take every thought captive? How can we best resist the devil so he will flee from us?

[Discover more about controlling our thoughts in Philippians 4:8, Colossians 3:2, and 1 John 4:4.]

DAY 38: DEVOTED TO JESUS
2 CORINTHIANS 11:1–33

But I am afraid that just as Eve was deceived by the serpent's cunning, your minds may somehow be led astray from your sincere and pure devotion to Christ. (2 Corinthians 11:3)

In Chapter 23, "Alive in Jesus," we see Paul placing the blame for humanity's fall on Adam. In the above passage, however, Paul focuses on Eve's role in the couple's disobedience to their creator's command. He says plainly that the serpent's cunning deceived Eve.

Paul worries that in the same way the church in Corinth might also diverge from their faith—that they'll go astray by following the wrong influences of others, thereby ditching their devotion to Jesus.

He doesn't share the source of this deception. But the threat could arise from false teachers who misrepresent Jesus, the devil's cunning schemes, or both.

Paul fears this outcome for the church in Corinth. This is despite the eighteen months he spent with them, a subsequent visit, his prayers, and his letters of instruction to them. He has invested much into them, yet he's afraid they'll veer off track. If, after all this, Paul carries this unease about them, we too should guard against influences that could lead us astray.

This isn't an issue of them walking away from their faith. Instead, Paul is concerned that these negative influences will detract from their "sincere and pure devotion" to Jesus.

The word devotion only occurs one other time in the New Testament. You might already suspect where. It appears in Paul's other letter to his friends in Corinth. This time he urges them to live with an "undivided devotion to the Lord" (1 Corinthians 7:35).

Merging these two related verses, we get a sense that our devotion to Jesus should be sincere, pure, and undivided. The opposite of this is insincere, impure, and divided. This gives us a sense of

Love Is Patient

incomplete devotion, a partial commitment to following Jesus. It's unacceptable.

When we believe in Jesus and follow him, he wants us to go all in. There is no looking back (Genesis 19:23–26 and Luke 9:62). God deserves our complete devotion for the rest of our lives. We must reject anything or anyone that distracts us from him.

Are we fully devoted to Jesus, or only partially so? What influences must we remove from our life that threaten to distract us from our dedication to our Savior?

[Discover more about devotion to Jesus in Matthew 6:24, Hebrews 10:36–39, and 1 John 1:6–7.]

DIG DEEPER: FALSE TEACHERS

For such people are false apostles, deceitful workers, masquerading as apostles of Christ. (2 Corinthians 11:13)

Not long after Paul's concern about an ungodly influence leading the people in the Corinthian church astray, we read this threat about false teachers. Given the context, we can connect these two verses, concluding that Paul worries false teachers will weaken the church's devotion to Jesus.

Paul speaks of false prophets. Though they work in the kingdom of God, their actions carry deception. Their goals run counter to Jesus's. They are pretend apostles.

Just as Jesus's followers in Corinth must shield themselves from those who masquerade as good, so too should we. Though we are wise to guard against ungodly influences outside the church, the warning here is to watch out for those on the inside who could lead us astray.

This may be in the form of outright heresy, or it could be from teachers who tack on unbiblical requirements for our faith journey. Following Jesus is enough. We need do nothing more to be his disciples and receive eternal life. Don't let anyone add to Jesus's good news or pile on requirements to what it means to believe in him.

We should follow the example of the Jews in Berea, who eagerly receive Paul's teaching and then examine the Scriptures to verify that he spoke truth (Acts 17:11).

What teachings have we accepted that go beyond what the Bible says? Are there teachers we should stop listening to?

[Discover more about false teachers in 1 Timothy 1:3, 1 Timothy 6:3–5, 2 Timothy 2:14–19, and 2 Peter 2:1–3.]

DAY 39: PAUL'S THORN IN THE FLESH
2 CORINTHIANS 12:1–10

Therefore, in order to keep me from becoming conceited, I was given a thorn in my flesh, a messenger of Satan, to torment me. (2 Corinthians 12:7)

Paul tells the Corinthian church about an experience he had of going to the third heaven. He's not sure if his body went there or just his spirit. The encounter so humbles him that he even describes this event in the third person, although we later realize he's talking about himself.

Bible scholars debate what this third heaven refers to, but a simple understanding comes from examining the other times Scripture uses the word *heaven*.

Sometimes heaven means the atmosphere, the sky we see when we look up. We can understand this as the first meaning of heaven (Acts 14:17).

Other times heaven refers to the cosmos, to the starry space that surrounds our planet. This is the second use of heaven (Psalm 19:4–6).

The third occurrence refers to God's heavenly home and our future paradise, where we'll live with him forever. This is the third use of heaven (Matthew 5:16). This stands as the simplest understanding of what Paul means by the third heaven.

Next, Paul isn't sure what part of him went to heaven. Was it his entire body or did he have an out-of-body experience, with just his spirit going there? Since he's not sure, we can't be sure either. But we shouldn't let this distract us from the fact that Paul went to heaven for a time and then returned to his life here on earth.

What Paul experienced in heaven is for him alone and not for us. Therefore, he doesn't share it. In fact, God prohibits him from doing so. Though I'd like to know this message—and you may too— we must accept that it only concerns Paul.

Paul has every reason to boast in his experience.

Love Is Patient

But this could become an unhealthy pride in what the Almighty did by bringing him into the third heaven and revealing truth to him.

To keep him in check, Paul received a thorn in the flesh. He doesn't specify what this is, and we can only speculate. Therefore, it accomplishes nothing to list the possibilities, though since Paul uses the word flesh, we can assume it's a physical condition and not spiritual. What's important is that this issue vexed him terribly, and it may have affected his ability to minister to others.

Paul clearly states that this assault comes from Satan, not God. Yet Paul also says this was *given to* him, not *afflicted upon* him. Since the enemy afflicts and God gives, does this mean God was behind it? Though a distressing thought, let's remember Job. God did not afflict Job, but merely permitted Satan to do so. The same scenario fits with Paul, so let's not criticize God and his sovereignty. Instead, place the blame on Satan, where it belongs.

Three times Paul begs God to remove his thorn in the flesh. It seems like a logical request for God to take away this affliction that affects Paul's life and impacts his ministry. Yet the Almighty declines. He tells Paul that his grace is enough, that he can better accomplish his purpose through Paul's weakness and keeping his servant's conceit in check.

Though Paul's thorn in the flesh is a perplexing concern to every follower of Jesus, we know that pride is the reason behind it. We will do well then to keep our pride in check and not boast about ourselves.

What should we do to keep our pride in check? When difficulties assail us, do we blame God or Satan?

[Discover more about pride in Proverbs 16:18, James 1:9–10, and 1 John 2:16.]

DIG DEEPER: ENCOURAGE ONE ANOTHER

Strive for full restoration, encourage one another, be of one mind, live in peace. (2 Corinthians 13:11)

Scripture gives us many commands about how we are to treat one another. The one given most often is to love one another. The command to encourage one another also occurs multiple times. One of these passages is here in 2 Corinthians.

Offering encouragement is often a result of the intentional action to make our words count, celebrating Jesus and inspiring one another. It's bypassing easy, socially acceptable interactions about family, work, sports, and weather. It's skipping trivial exchanges to embrace a dialogue full of purpose.

Offering encouragement takes work, but it's worth the effort.

One of the best ways we can support each other is through our words. For this encouragement to have the deepest impact, it must be both meaningful and spiritual. When we rightly encourage one another, we point people to Jesus. This may occur directly or indirectly, but it is intentional.

May we seek to encourage each other every day.

What can we do to encourage one another? Who might we encourage today?

[Discover more about encouraging one another in 1 Thessalonians 4:18, 1 Thessalonians 5:11, and Hebrews 3:13.]

DAY 40: PAUL'S BLESSING
2 CORINTHIANS 12:11–13:14

May the grace of the Lord Jesus Christ, and the love of God, and the fellowship of the Holy Spirit be with you all.
(2 Corinthians 13:14)

In Chapter 35, "Generosity," we looked at Paul's affirmation of the people at the church in Corinth by listing six things that they excel at. This is an affirming verse given their many struggles. Yet in Chapter 38, "Devoted to Jesus," we saw Paul share his fear that an outside influence will lead them astray from their total devotion to Jesus.

Now Paul reveals another concern he has for this struggling congregation. He's afraid that when he arrives for his visit, he'll find "discord, jealousy, fits of rage, selfish ambition, slander, gossip, arrogance and disorder" (2 Corinthians 12:20).

If the Corinthians took solace in Paul's earlier affirmation of them, his worry over them losing their devotion to God would certainly give them pause. Yet this list of seven negative traits emerges as most distressing, even though it seems a likely outcome given this church's many struggles.

Fortunately, Paul doesn't end his letter with warnings and concerns. Instead, he leaves them with a most uplifting blessing. This is his final written word to them and serves as his parting benediction of hope for a better future.

This blessing covers a trio of godly traits, each one coming from one person of the Trinity.

First, Paul blesses them with grace from Jesus. Grace is receiving good things that we don't deserve. Our right standing with God through Jesus's sacrificial death and resurrection is the greatest offer of grace anyone could ever receive.

Next, Paul blesses them with love from Father God. We talked about how we are to love one another in Chapter 20, "The Greatest of These Is Love." Now consider this description of love's traits coming from our Heavenly Father, who provides

Love Is Patient

them in full perfection, through everlasting patience, and without limit. How comforting.

Third, Paul blesses them with the fellowship of the Holy Spirit. When Jesus returned to heaven, Father God sent the Holy Spirit to Jesus's followers. The Holy Spirit guides them, teaches them, and instructs them. Beyond this, Paul wants the Corinthians to enjoy fellowship with the Holy Spirit. Paul desires they connect with God's Spirit and walk with him every day and in all they do.

Though written to the church in Corinth, we can claim this blessing as our own to receive Jesus's grace, our Heavenly Father's love, and the Holy Spirit's fellowship.

How can this blessing encourage us in our daily living? In what ways can we bless others, as Paul blessed the Corinthians?

[Discover three more blessings from Paul in Romans 1:7, Ephesians 3:20–21, and 1 Thessalonians 5:23. Read another blessing in Numbers 6:24–26.]

If you liked *Love Is Patient*, please leave a review online. Your review will help others discover this book and encourage them to read it too.

Thank you.

WHAT BOOK DO YOU WANT TO READ NEXT?

Consider these other books in the 40-Day Bible Study Series:

- Dear Theophilus (the Gospel of **Luke**, formerly That You May Know)
- Dear Theophilus, **Acts** (formerly Tongues of Fire)
- Dear Theophilus, **Isaiah** (formerly For Unto Us)
- Dear Theophilus, **Minor Prophets** (formerly Return to Me)
- Dear Theophilus, **Job** (formerly I Hope in Him)
- Living Water (**John**)

What Book Do You Want to Read Next?

- A New Heaven and a New Earth (**Revelation**)
- Love One Another (**1, 2, and 3 John**)
- Run with Perseverance (**Hebrews**)
- James and Jude Bible Study
- Matthew Bible Study
- 1 & 2 Peter Bible Study
- Mark Bible Study (available in 2025)

FOR SMALL GROUPS, SUNDAY SCHOOL, AND CLASSES

Love Is Patient makes an ideal eight-week Bible study discussion guide for small groups, Sunday School, and classes. In preparation for the conversation, read one chapter of this book each weekday, Monday through Friday.

- Week 1: read 1 through 5.
- Week 2: read 6 through 10.
- Week 3: read 11 through 15.
- Week 4: read 16 through 20.
- Week 5: read 21 through 25.
- Week 6: read 26 through 30.
- Week 7: read 31 through 35.
- Week 8: read 36 through 40.

For Small Groups, Sunday School, and Classes

When you get together, discuss the questions at the end of each chapter. The leader can use all the questions to guide this discussion or pick which ones to focus on.

Before beginning the discussion, pray as a group. Ask for Holy Spirit insight and clarity.

As you consider each chapter's questions:

As you consider each chapter's questions:

- Look for how this can grow your understanding of the Bible.
- Evaluate how this can expand your faith perspective.
- Consider what you need to change in how you live your lives.

End by asking God to help apply what you've learned.

May God bless you as you read and study his word.

IF YOU'RE NEW TO THE BIBLE

Each entry in this book contains Bible references. These can guide you if you want to learn more. If you're not familiar with the Bible, here's an overview to get you started, give some context, and minimize confusion.

First, the Bible is a collection of works written by various authors over several centuries. Think of the Bible as a diverse anthology of godly communication. It contains historical accounts, poetry, songs, letters of instruction and encouragement, messages from God sent through his representatives, and prophecies.

Most versions of the Bible have sixty-six books grouped into two sections: The Old Testament and the New Testament. The Old Testament contains thirty-nine books that precede and anticipate Jesus. The New Testament includes twenty-seven books and covers Jesus's life and the work of his followers.

The reference notations in the Bible, such as Romans 3:23, are analogous to line numbers in a Shakespearean play. They serve as a study aid. Since the Bible is much longer and more complex than a play, its reference notations are more involved.

As already mentioned, the Bible is an amalgam of books, or sections, such as Genesis, Psalms, or 1 Peter. These are the names given to them, over time, based on the piece's author, audience, or purpose.

In the 1200s, each book was divided into chapters, such as Acts 2 or Psalm 23. In the 1500s, the chapters were further subdivided into verses, such as John 3:16. Let's use this as an example.

The name of the book (John) appears first, followed by the chapter number (3), a colon, and then the verse number (16). Sometimes called a chapter-verse reference notation, this helps people quickly find a specific text regardless of their version of the Bible.

Although the goal was to place these chapter and verse divisions at logical breaks, they sometimes

If You're New to the Bible

seem arbitrary. Therefore, it's good practice to read what precedes and follows each passage you're studying. The text before or after it may contain relevant insights into the portion you're exploring.

Here's how to look up a specific passage in the Bible based on its reference: Most Bibles contain a table of contents, which gives the page number for the beginning of each book. Start there. Locate the book you want to read, and turn to that page. Then flip forward to the chapter you want. Last, skim that chapter to locate the specific verse.

If you want to read online, enter the reference into BibleGateway.com or BibleHub.com. Also check out the YouVersion app.

Learn more about the greatest book ever written at ABibleADay.com, which provides a Bible blog, summaries of the books of the Bible, a dictionary of Bible terms, Bible reading plans, and other resources.

ABOUT PETER DEHAAN

Peter DeHaan, PhD, wants to change the world one word at a time. His books and blog posts discuss God, the Bible, and church, geared toward spiritual seekers and church dropouts. Many people feel church has let them down, and Peter seeks to encourage them as they search for a place to belong.

But he's not afraid to ask tough questions or make religious people squirm. He's not trying to be provocative. Instead, he seeks truth, even if it makes people uncomfortable. Peter urges Christians to push past the status quo and reexamine how they practice their faith in every part of their lives.

Peter earned his doctorate, awarded with high distinction, from Trinity College of the Bible and Theological Seminary. He lives with his wife in beautiful Southwest Michigan and wrangles crossword puzzles in his spare time.

A lifelong student of Scripture, Peter wrote the 1,000-page website ABibleADay.com to encourage people to explore the Bible, the greatest book ever written. His popular blog, at PeterDeHaan.com, addresses biblical Christianity to build a faith that matters.

Read his blog, receive his newsletter, and learn more at PeterDeHaan.com.

BOOKS BY PETER DEHAAN

40-Day Bible Study Series

Dear Theophilus (the Gospel of Luke, formerly That You May Know)

Dear Theophilus, Acts (formerly Tongues of Fire)

Dear Theophilus, Isaiah (formerly For Unto Us)

Dear Theophilus, Minor Prophets (formerly Return to Me)

Dear Theophilus, Job (formerly I Hope in Him)

Living Water (the Gospel of John)

Love Is Patient (Paul's letters to the Corinthians)

A New Heaven and a New Earth (John's Revelation)

Love One Another (John's letters)

Run with Perseverance (the book of Hebrews)

James and Jude Bible Study

Matthew Bible Study

1 & 2 Peter Bible Study

Mark Bible Study (available in 2025)

Holiday Celebration Bible Study Series

The Advent of Jesus (an Advent devotional)

The Ministry of Jesus (an Ordinary Time devotional)

The Passion of Jesus (a Lenten devotional)

The Victory of Jesus (an Easter devotional)

Bible Character Sketches Series

Women of the Bible

The Friends and Foes of Jesus

Old Testament Sinners and Saints

More Old Testament Sinners and Saints

Visiting Churches Series

Shopping for Church

Visiting Online Church

52 Churches

The 52 Churches Workbook

More Than 52 Churches

The More Than 52 Churches Workbook

Other Books

Jesus's Broken Church

Martin Luther's 95 Theses

The Christian Church's LGBTQ Failure

Bridging the Sacred-Secular Divide

Beyond Psalm 150

How Big Is Your Tent?

For the latest list of all Peter's books, go to PeterDeHaan.com/books.

www.ingramcontent.com/pod-product-compliance
Lightning Source LLC
Chambersburg PA
CBHW072004110526
44592CB00012B/1201